PURE BREED
POULTRY RAISING

Large fowl—soft feather—light breed—white Leghorn cockerel

Large fowl—soft feather—light breed—white leghorn pullet

PURE BREED POULTRY RAISING

RICK KEMP

Kangaroo Press

To my wife Sandra and my daughters,
Nicole and Emily

Cover: *Bantam—soft feather—Ancona male*

Reprinted with corrections in 1987 and 1994
First published in 1985 by Kangaroo Press Pty Ltd
3 Whitehall Road Kenthurst 2156
PO Box 6125 Dural Delivery Centre NSW 2158 Australia
Typeset by G.T. Setters Pty Limited
Printed in Singapore by
Singapore National Printers Ltd

ISBN 0 86417 058 0

Contents

Acknowledgements

To my wife, Sandra, for her constructive comments and review of the book.
To my parents Al and Kit who thought I was rid of the 'chook bug' when I went to boarding school.
To my agriculture students both past and present. They opened my eyes to the difficulties and disappointments of the novice poultry raiser.
To Mr Allan Sharpe of Griffith, the long standing Chief Steward of the Griffith Show Poultry Pavilion for his practical and down to earth poultry advice.
To Mr Bert E. Brown, to whom the Poultry Pavilion at Griffith has been dedicated, for his fascinating historical background on many of poultry's legendary breeders and for his pile of *Poultry* newspapers.
To the late Les Collis for his hours of inspirational talk particularly on White Leghorns.
To the Poultry Fancy in general for the satisfying times it has given me.

Introduction

In recent years, we have seen a change in our society's attitude to poultry raising. It has re-established itself as a worthwhile leisure time activity. We have passed through an era where it was unfashionable to keep fowls just as it was unfashionable to grow vegetables in the backyard. Fortunately for poultry raising, times have changed and it is now regarded as quite acceptable, even 'trendy' to indulge in such activities. This has been aided by the rapid growth and acceptance of hobby farming activities.

As a result, we have a generation of children, products of parents that have not engaged in these activities themselves. As a consequence, even if the youngster is interested in poultry raising, the traditional parent hand down source of knowledge does not exist to help him. The result is the child has been deprived of rich experiences that were regarded as part of growing up many years ago.

Coupled with this has been a vast change in poultry technology geared to the commercial output of eggs and chicken meat. The roast fowl reserved for special events of the 1950s for example birthdays, Christmas and Easter is now no longer the luxury it used to be. In fact chicken meat is now regarded as part of our staple diet and one of the few meat sources showing an increase in consumption with its adaptability to the take away food industry. This is a direct product of the ever improving poultry technology. The technology has rubbed off on the backyard and hobby farm poultry raiser, so the fowl yard of the 1950s is not the one used by the poultry fancier of the 1990s.

Being involved in pure breed poultry raising, the individual is helping preserve an important gene pool that can be drawn upon by the modern poultry geneticist in the quest for developing newer and commercially more efficient hybrids.

To overcome the dual problems brought about by social and technological change, this book has been written. Having been privileged to live through and be part of this change in the poultry world, I now feel that it is time to make a literary contribution to that which has given me such personal pleasure.

The book's purpose is to give a simple and straight forward formula or 'recipe' which a beginner or novice can confidently use to successfully breed, raise and exhibit pure breed poultry. It is a formula that can be built upon as interest grows and time passes. Much of this book's contents will also prove useful to the old hands at the game, with sufficient depth of treatment that it can be frequently referred back to.

In NSW, agriculture as a subject has been moved into the Technology and Applied Science Key Learning Area. With relatively little expense and space, a poultry unit can be established in the school situation. Whilst this book is not written in the traditional text book form, its style allows ideas for design projects to flow naturally from the material.

The poultry raising formula developed in this book is a result of eighteen years teaching agriculture and an interest since childhood in pure breed poultry raising. Its development takes into account the many mistakes and disappointments experienced personally and by young people trying to come to grips with pure breed poultry raising. To my students I owe a debt as they have opened my eyes to many problems I had not previously noticed.

To those new to the world of pure breed poultry raising (the poultry fancy), a warm welcome to a satisfying educational leisure time activity.

Large fowl—soft feather—heavy breed—light Sussex cockerel

Large fowl—soft feather—heavy breed—light Sussex pullet

1 History of Pure Breed Poultry

Birds have always provided a source of food since the early beginnings of man. They were trapped, hunted and their nests raided. Most experts agree that the forerunners of the modern races of domestic fowl are the native jungle fowls of the Indian subcontinent.

The evolution of the domestic fowl has been hastened by the process of artificial selection. Fowls were selected for:

1. Egg laying
2. Flesh quality and quantity
3. Cock fighting ability
4. General appearance.

The last (4) has only assumed importance to European poultry keepers in the last one hundred and fifty years. Only a limited number of breeds have been known for more than five to six hundred years and most of the modern breeds as we know them today have been created since Victorian times (1840s to 1900).

Four wild fowls existed in the Indian subcontinent:

1. Red Jungle Fowl
2. Grey Jungle Fowl
3. Ceylon Jungle Fowl
4. Javan Jungle Fowl

Their distribution is shown on Map 1. It is commonly held that the Red Jungle Fowl was the native fowl from which the Indians developed the early domestic fowl as far back as 3-4000 B.C. Cock fighting was a major influence on its development. The most famous of the Indian fighting fowls was the Asil. It was developed by the early princes of India and had the following features:

1. Broad chested
2. Hard close feathers
3. Heavy weight
4. Clean legged (no feathers on legs)
5. Pea comb.

There was a system of five classes of Asils based on a caste system with the top belonging to royalty and the lowest belonging to the lowest members of society.

Map 1

In the Malay Archipelego, the Malay Game was also developed about the same time. The Malay was used much later in the development of many of the modern breeds of fowls.

The Japanese were also active at this time developing a large heavyweight game fowl of which the Shamo and Tuzo are examples.

The region is accredited with giving us the word bantam which is believed to have originated from the Javanese *ban tom* meaning 'small fowl'.

Fowls had been domesticated in China by 1400 B.C. during the Shang Dynasty. The Chinese had also developed crude incubators for hatching hundreds of eggs at a time.

The Ancient Egyptians had domesticated wild fowl for the production of eggs and meat before Christ. They also built large oven-like incubators that were capable of hatching thousands of eggs at a time. A man was placed inside to control incubating conditions during the hatch.

Fowls were reported in Babylon as early as 700 B.C.

Invading armies were responsible for the westward spread of the Red Jungle Fowl's descendants to Europe (refer to Map 2). Following their conquest of India Persian soldiers took Indian fowls home with them in 600 B.C. They were quick to realise their value as sport and as food.

The fowl first appeared in Europe about 500 B.C. when Alexander the Great conquered Persia. The Greeks became captivated with cock fighting as a sport. In fact, the sport became so popular, the National Cockfighting Championships became part of the ancient Olympic Games.

The Romans willingly accepted the fowl and carried it with the expansion of the Roman Empire. Caesar had made fowl part of his banquet fare. So far had the Romans spread the fowl through their trading Empire that by 55 B.C. the Britons were practising cock fighting at the time of Julius Caesar's landing.

The fighting cock had been accepted as symbol of courage for all soldiers.

During the Middle Ages major races of fowls started to develop in three relatively isolated and different regions (refer to Map 3). These were:

1. Mediterranean fowls
2. Asian Game fowls
3. Asian Soft Feather fowls.

The Mediterranean fowls are often referred to as Light Breeds with the following features:

1. Seldom go broody
2. Lay pure white eggs
3. Have white ear lobes
4. Have large combs—regarded as a delicacy.

This race of fowls are the forerunners of the Leghorns, Minorcas, Andalusians and Anconas of today.

The Asian Game Fowls developed along different lines with the following features:

1. Hardest and tightest feathering of all breeds

Map 2

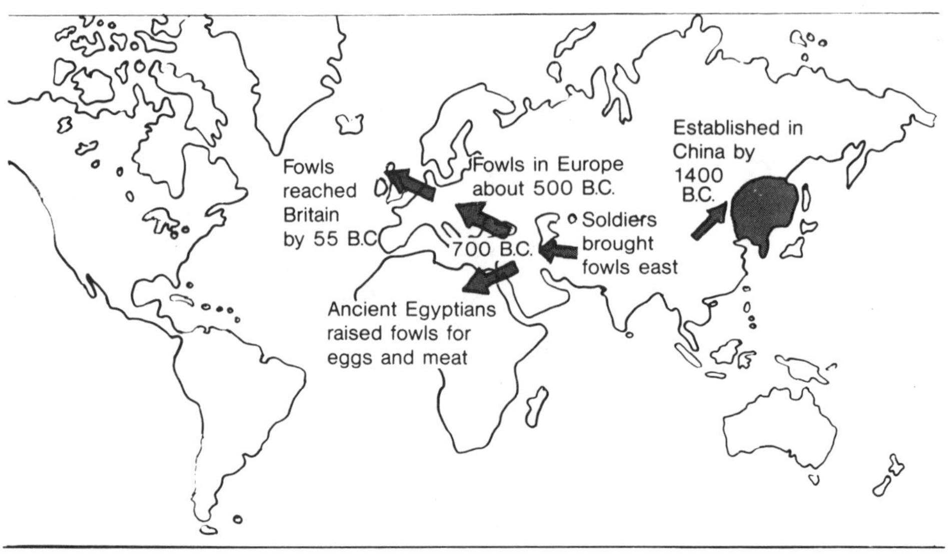

Map 3

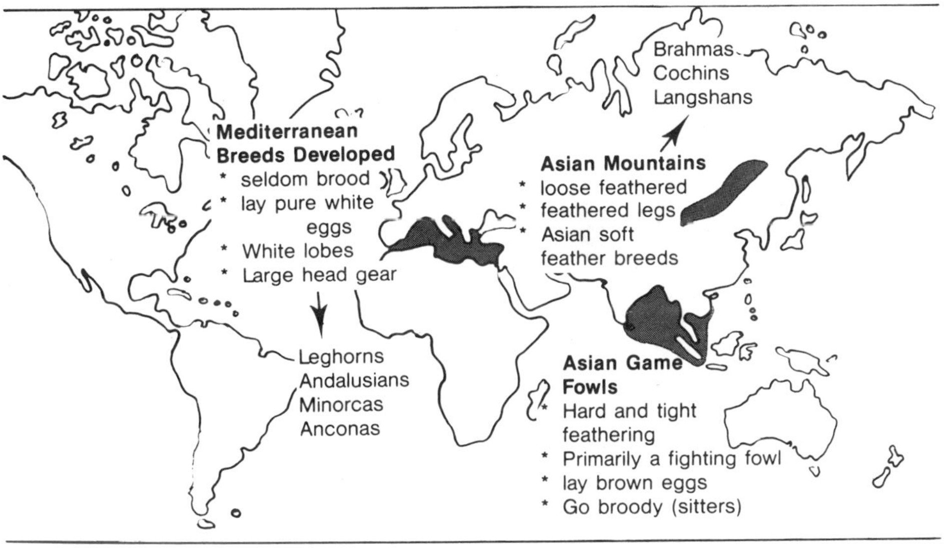

2. Primarily a fighting fowl
3. Lay brown eggs
4. Go broody (sitters).

The Asian Softfeather fowls developed in the mountain regions of Asia and these feature:

1. Looser and softer feathers
2. Feathered legs.

Examples of this race of fowls include the Brahma, Cochin and Langshan.

Columbus was responsible for the introduction of the fowl to America where it naturalised very quickly.

The period 1800–1859 was marked by a number of important events that inspired what many call the 'Golden Age of pure breed poultry'. These events were:

1. The work of Robert Bakewell of Dishley on selective breeding to develop new breeds of animals
2. The work of Charles Darwin, particularly with regard to the transmission of traits from one generation to the next
3. The fashionable Victorian pastime of deliberately creating new varieties of animals.

In 1865, to cope with the range of new varieties of fowls being created, the Poultry Club of Great Britain published the first *Standard of Excellence in Exhibition Poultry.* Exhibition poultry became very fashionable and financially rewarding. Many famous names emerged during this period including:

1. **Sir John Sebright** originator of the Sebright bantam
2. **William Tegetmeier** editor of the *Standard of Excellence in Exhibition Poultry*
3. **William Cook** originator of the Orpington breed, ancestor of the Australorp
4. **Lewis Wright** known for his Brahma fowls and *Illustrated Book of Poultry* which is still available today through a recent reprinting.

New breeds of fowls were developed during this time by crossing the Mediterranean, Asian Game and Asian Softfeather races of fowls. The new breeds, many of which are still popular today can be grouped as follows:

1. **English breeds** for example the Dorking, Sussex and Orpington all of which have white skin and legs.
2. **American breeds** for example the Plymouth Rock, Wyandotte, Rhode Island and Jersey Giant distinguished by their yellow pigmentation.
3. **European breeds** for example the Welsummer, Barnevelder and Appenzuller. These lay brown eggs.

The distribution of these breeds is shown on Map 4.

Two directions began to evolve:

1. The poultry farm based on the existing breeds eg. Leghorns for eggs and Sussex for meat.
2. The acceptance of the newer strains and hybrids based on the evolving science of genetics.

Map 4

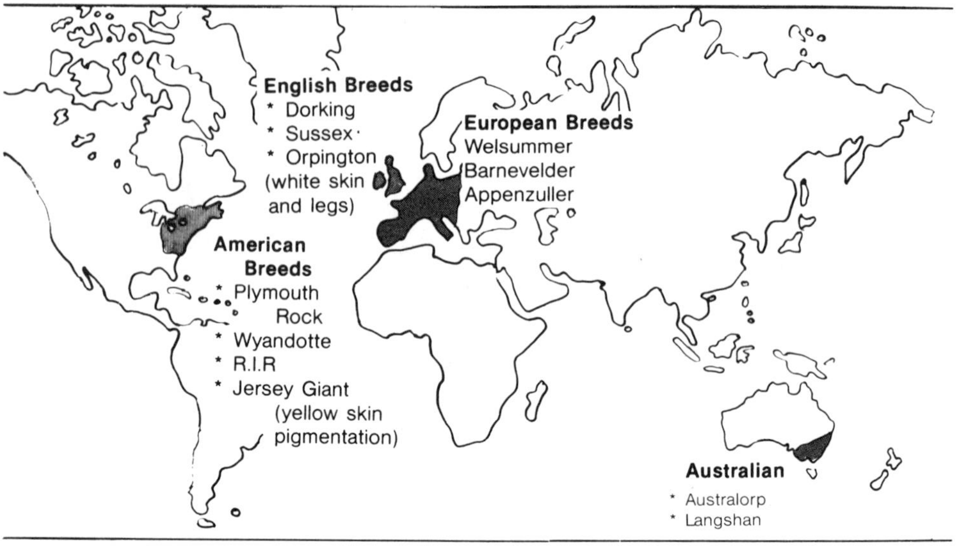

William Bateson working with poultry verified many of Mendel's findings. He was later joined by Punnett. Punnett continued to work on poultry genetics for the next fifty years and was instrumental in applying poultry genetics to food production during the First World War, when serving in the Food Production Department of the British Board of Agriculture.

By the end of the Second World War, the value of the cross breed or hybrid fowl in commercial production was established. The modern commercial fowl is a cross bred fowl, developed into two distinct types:

1. Egg laying
2. Meat production.

They are selected only for their productivity and very little attention is paid to their appearance.

Pure breeds in Australia

Fowls were brought to Australia by the early European settlers but little appears to have been recorded as to what breeds were imported and from where.

Game fowls were known to have been imported early, as cockfighting existed as a sport in the very early 1800s. Evidence of such activities were recorded in the newspapers of the day.

Records held by the Royal Agricultural Society of N.S.W. indicate that the Dorking, Hamburgh and Game breeds were being bred and exhibited by the mid 1800s. As the various American, British and European utility breeds by Plymouth Rock, Orpingtons and Faverolles were developed and showed some commercial advantage over existing breeds, they were soon imported.

A clear division in the poultry ranks soon emerged. There were those who assessed breeds purely in commercial advantage and those described as fancy fowl breeders who were prepared to forego utility performance in favour of breed beauty. Added to this, many of the second group became pre-occupied with exaggeration of fancy points such as colour, combs, lobes and size at the expense of the breed's original utility performance. The end result was that many breeds were radically altered in appearance and greatly diminished in numbers, in some cases, disappearing altogether.

Australian breeders also set about developing their own breeds. The earliest efforts were directed towards Game fowls with the development of the Australian Pit Game and Australian Game breeds. It was some time later that two Australian breeds were developed, the Australorp and the Chinese Langshan. Both breeds were good commercial layers but also produced a useful meat carcase.

The opening of quarantine facilities may see a resurgence of interest in pure breed poultry as an opportunity will then exist to import many breeds that have not been seen in this country or have become extinct following many years of breeder disinterest.

2 Pure Breeds of Poultry

Fowls as we know them in Australia can be grouped as follows:

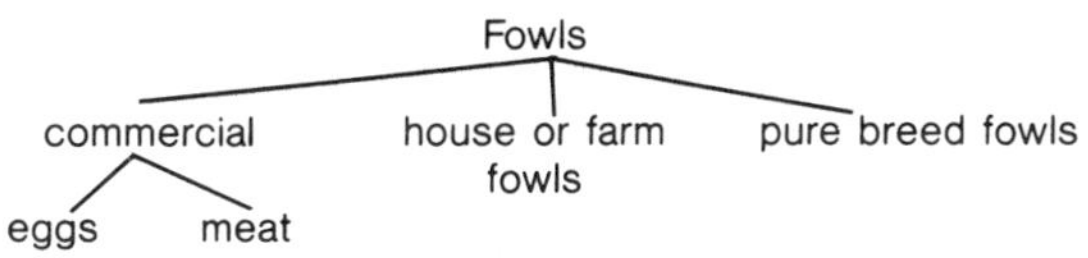

Let's now look at each of these groups of fowls.

Commercial

Numerically, by far, the largest group. They have been carefully developed by geneticists from existing pure breed fowls to maximise production of meat or eggs. They are elaborate cross breeds or hybrids that have been developed into two distinctively different types.

Egg Laying Egg laying ability and persistency of laying have been bred into these birds by using specially selected lines of fowls. Mostly they are the products of the White Leghorn male and Australorp female cross. Another breed used in the laying cross is the New Hampshire. Many of these fowls are sold by commercial hatcheries under special names, for example Hy-Line Superlayer and Brinkkotter strains from Victoria. These fowls are kept until they are between 72 and 104 weeks of age and then disposed of.

Meat These are special cross breeds or hybrids that have been selected for rapid growth and high food conversion. They are processed for eating at 6 to 8 weeks of age and have been responsible for changing the luxury of the 1950s roast fowl into an economical everyday meat source of the 1990s. These fowls are termed broilers with both male and female being eaten.

House or farm fowls

This is a group or category of convenience that the author has included to cover most of the fowls found around the home or farm. They may be of one breed but not selected and bred to a recognised poultry breed standard, or they may be a random cross breed, as often their keeper brings in a new rooster of a different breed each year to 'liven up' the offspring.

Pure breed fowls

This is the group to which this book addresses itself. 'Pure breed' fowls refers to the fowls that have been bred and selected to conform as closely as possible to the standards that have been written for each breed. Most in Australia follow the standards as set out in the British Poultry Standard recognised by the Poultry Club of Great Britain. A similar standard exists in the United States of America called the *Standard of Perfection* printed by the American Poultry Association.

Pure breed fowls can be further classified into the groups shown in the table overleaf; breed examples are listed under each.

Terms arising from the classifications

Hard feather These are often called game fowls. Their origin goes back to the fowls that were bred for cock fighting. This is illegal in Australia but is still practised in Asia and some states of America. Locally, they are regarded as exhibition fowls only. The feathers tightly and closely follow the contour of the body.

Soft feather The British Poultry Standard defines soft feather as 'applied to breeds other

Pure breed fowls

Bred to a standard

- **large fowls**
  - **hard feather**
    - Asil
    - Australian Game
    - Australian Pit Game
    - Indian Game
    - Malay Game
    - Old English Game
    - Shamo
  - **soft feather**
    - **light breeds**
      - Leghorn
      - Minorca
      - Ancona
      - Andalusian
      - Hamburgh
      - Campine
      - Poland
      - Silkie
      - Welsummer
      - Araucana
    - **heavy breeds**
      - Australorp
      - Barnevelder
      - Brahma
      - Dorking
      - Faverolles
      - Langshan
      - New Hampshire
      - Orpington
      - Plymouth Rock
      - Rhode Island
      - Sussex
      - Wyandotte
- **bantam**
  - **hard feather**
    - Asil
    - Indian Game
    - Malay Game
    - Old English Game
    - Modern Game
  - **soft feather**
    - Australorp
    - Ancona
    - Frizzle
    - Japanese
    - Langshan
    - Leghorn
    - Pekin
    - Rosecomb
    - Rhode Island
    - Sussex
    - Sebright
    - Wyandotte

than the hard feather or game group'. Most are much looser in feathering and have a distinct softness of feel.

Light breeds These fowls have a characteristic lightness of frame with an accompanying lightness of muscle when compared to heavy breeds. Often they are tighter in feathering than heavy breeds.

Heavy breeds Generally heavily framed (boned) with well developed muscling. Have a characteristic heavy appearance.

Large fowl—soft feather—Australorp male

Bantam—soft feather—Australorp cockerel

Large fowl—soft feather—Chinese Langshan cock

Bantam—hard feather—Old English Game blue red light leg female

Bantam—hard feather—Old English Game blue tail wheaten pullet

Bantam—hard feather—Old English Game wheaten female

Bantam—hard feather—Old English Game blue red dark leg pullet

Bantam—hard feather—Old English Game blue red dark leg cockerel

Bantam—hard feather—Modern Game black red dark leg cockerel

Breed characteristics summary

Large fowls—hard feather

breed	*origin*	*colour*	*egg colour*	*comment*
Asil	Asia—India	Light Red Dark Red Red Wheaten	Tinted	Oldest game fowl breed. Not seen in Australia
Australian Game	Australia	Variable Hen feathered males seen	Tinted	Often exhibited under weights. Both breeds in hands of staunch devotees
Australian Pit Game	Australia	Black Red Duckwing Pile White	Tinted	

breed	*origin*	*colour*	*egg colour*	*comment*
Indian Game	Great Britain	Cornish (dark) Blue Jubilee	Tinted	Developed from Asil, Old English Game and Malay Game. Huge breasts and thighs
Malay Game	Asia	Black Black Red Pile Spangle White	Tinted	Very old breed
Old English Game	Britain	Over 30 colours known. Main colours include Black, Blue, Black Red, Pile Duckwing, Crele Spangle	Tinted	Origins go back to the Roman invasion of England
Shamo	Asia—Japan	Any of the above game colours	Tinted	Not seen in Australian shows

Large fowls—soft feather—light breeds

breed	*origin*	*colour*	*egg colour*	*comment*
1. Leghorn	Italy	12 colours common inc. Black, Brown, Blue, White	White	Top laying breed. Still very popular
2. Minorca	Spain	Black, White, Blue	White	Rare but still have a few staunch devotees
3. Ancona	Italy	Black with beetle green sheen. Each feather has a white 'V' strip	White to cream	Popular exhibition fowl with a strong breed club
4. Andalusian	Spain	Exhibition birds Blue	White	Often quoted as an example of incomplete dominance of colour in genetics
5. Hamburgh	Northern Europe	Black, Gold, and Silver Pencilled, Silver Spangled	White	Purely exhibition fowl. Rose comb
6. Campine	Belgium	Beetle green barring over gold or silver ground colour	White	Major role in work on autosexing breeds

breed	origin	colour	egg colour	comment
7. Poland	Poland	Gold, Silver, White, White Crested Blue, Cuckoo, Black, Chamois	White	Very old breed
8. Silkie	Asia—origin in doubt, either India, China, Japan	Many—common colours, White, Black, Gold, Blue, Silver, Grey, Partridge	Tinted to cream	Persistent broodiness. Often used as broodies
9. Welsummer	Holland	Male—Black Red Female—Partridge	Brown to deep brown. Also mottled	Deep brown eggs have created much recent interest
10. Araucana	Chile	Any Old English Game colour. Lavender	Blue or green	Have built up a following because of their egg colour

1, 2, 3, and 4 also classified as Mediterranean breeds. 5, 6, 7, and 8 are regarded as purely exhibition fowls or 'fancy fowls'.

Large fowls—soft feather—heavy breeds

breed	origin	colour	egg colour	comment
Australorp	Australia	Black	Tinted to brown	Extremely popular
Barnevelder	Holland	Black, Double Laced, Partridge, Silver	Deep brown	Popular for its brown eggs
Brahma	Asia	Dark, Buff, Columbian, Light, White, Gold	Tinted	Rare in this country. Pea comb, feathered legs
Dorking	Great Britain	Cuckoo, White, Dark, Red, Silver Grey	Tinted	Five toed breed
Faverolles	France	Black, Salmon, Blue, Buff, White, Ermine	Tinted	Bearded fowls. Feathered legs. Five toed
Langshan	China	Black with beetle green sheen	Tinted to brown	Chinese variety more popular than Croad variety
New Hampshire	United States of America	Red	Tinted to brown	Bred by selection from the Rhode Island Red

breed	*origin*	*colour*	*egg colour*	*comment*
Orpington	Great Britain	Black, Buff, Blue, White	Brown	Used to develop the Australorp
Plymouth Rock	United States of America	Barred, Black, White, Buff, Columbian	Tinted	Barred factor used in sex linkage experiments
Rhode Island	United States of America	Red, White	Light brown to brown	A popular breed amongst rural people
Sussex	Great Britain	Light, Brown, Buff, White, Speckled, Silver	Tinted	A popular farm fowl with excellent table qualities
Wyandotte	United States	Barred, Black, Blue, Blue Laced, Buff, Buff Laced, Columbian, Red, Gold Laced, White, Silver Laced, Partridge, Silver Pencilled	Tinted	A good specimen still takes out top show awards. Rose comb. Popular amongst fanciers

Bantams—hard feather

Follow a similar description to their large fowl counterpart but smaller in size.

Bantams—soft feather

Where there is a large fowl counterpart refer to the large fowls description. The following table refers to bantams who do not have a large fowl equivalent or the large fowl equivalent is very rare in this country.

breed	*origin*	*colour*	*egg colour*	*comment*
Frizzle	Asia	Black, White Blue, Buff	White or tinted	Purely an exhibition variety
Japanese	Japan	Common colours Black Tailed White, White, Black, Grey Mottled, Blue	White or tinted	Carries lethal gene for short legs (creeper gene)
Pekin	Asia	Black, White, Blue, Cuckoo, Partridge	White or cream	Very old breed. Very popular on the show scene
Rosecomb	Great Britain	Black, Blue, White	White or cream	Exhibition fowl. A good specimen an eye catcher
Sebright	Great Britain	Gold, Silver	White or cream	Rose comb. Deliberately created exhibition bantam

As can be seen, there is a wide variety of pure breeds in the poultry world and it would be fair to say that there is a breed amongst the foregoing lists that would catch the eye of everybody. This is the appeal of pure breed poultry raising—the huge diversity.

This then brings us to the point of pure breed poultry versus cross breed poultry. If one is prepared to put in the time to keep cross breed poultry, then by taking on the pure breeds, a whole new dimension is opened up. Selecting the right breed will still ensure plenty of eggs, meat or both, as well as a new dimension in beauty and the challenge of breeding fowls to a standard.

In selecting a breed, the following points must be considered.

1. Which breed appeals to you.
2. Whether you want utilitarian fowls for meat, eggs or both, or whether you want a purely ornamental or fancy fowl.
3. Access to suitable stock. Care must be taken when opting for the rarer breeds as your choice of stock is limited. On the show front, you may find little competition giving you a hollow victory. However, you may find a calling in ensuring the survival of a rare breed and point (3) will be seen as an increased challenge.

Many breeders stay loyal to a breed for life whilst others enjoy the chance to change breeds once they feel they have mastered their earlier choice.

tam—hard feather—Indian Game male

Bantam—hard feather—Indian Game female

3 The External and Internal Features of the Fowl

The domestic fowl is part of the 8 600 species strong bird group which has managed to adapt to all but the high altitude frigid environments and to a complete underwater existence.

The bird group is distinguished from other animals by the following features:

1. Possess an external covering of feathers.
2. Possess a modified arm capable of allowing flight.
3. Walk on two legs (bipedal gait) that are covered in scales.
4. The first animal on the evolutionary tree to be warm blooded (homiothermic).
5. Reproduce by internal fertilisation with young developing in a hard shelled egg.
6. Breathe by lungs.
7. Have no teeth.
8. Possess a behaviour pattern that is mostly instinctive.

External appearance

The major external features of the fowl are presented in the diagram 'External features of the fowl'.

The features labelled are the ones most often used in the descriptions of pure breed fowls. In many cases, the parts are readily distinguishable by colour differences, or become obvious if an adult fowl is examined.

However the head of the fowl does need some further comment. It is often the head that can make or break a top exhibition fowl in the final analysis at judging time. The head parts are most exaggerated in the Mediterranean breeds of fowls with their large single comb, long wattles and stark white ear lobes against a red face.

The comb is a part of the fowl that has attracted breeders' and geneticists' interest over the years, and some of the many types seen include:

External features of the fowl

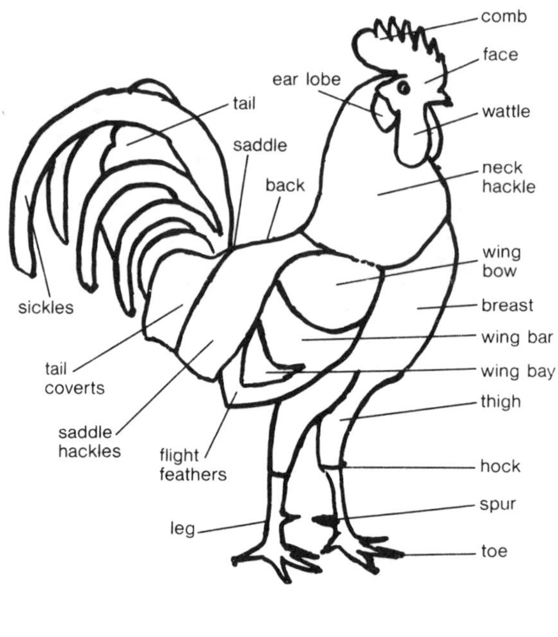

1. Single comb e.g. Leghorn, Australorp, Sussex
2. Rose comb e.g. Hamburgh, Wyandotte
3. Pea comb e.g. Brahma, Indian Game
4. Cushion comb e.g. Silkie
5. Leaf comb e.g. Houdan
6. Cup comb e.g. Sicilian Buttercup — Not seen in
7. Horn comb e.g. La Fleche — Australia

The eye colour is important in breed standards and once again the variation is wide. Some examples include:

1. Red e.g. Leghorns
2. Pearl e.g. Indian Game
3. Black e.g. Australorp, Silkie
4. Orange e.g. Light Sussex
5. Yellow e.g. Yellow Birchen Old English Game
6. Brown e.g. Duckwing Old English Game

The colour of the scales on the fowls' legs is also varied. As with a good clean head, a good pair of legs 'sets a fowl off' in appearance. Common leg colours include:

1. White e.g. Sussex
2. Yellow e.g. Leghorn, Rhode Island Red, Wyandotte
3. Willow or olive e.g. Old English Game Black Red
4. Grey e.g. Silkie
5. Black e.g. Australorp, Langshan
6. Blue e.g. Old English Game Blue
7. Mottled e.g. Ancona

A number of breeds derive their appeal from their feathered legs. This is generally an indication of the breeds' Asian Softfeather origin. The leg feathering ranges from the extremes of the Pekin bantams and the Silkie through to the Chinese Langshan and Faverolles.

Perhaps the most obvious and catching external feature of the fowl is its feathers. These can be grouped into three main categories according to their function.

1. Flight feathers
2. Contour or body shape feathers
3. Down feathers.

Let's now look at each group separately. Their location is indicated on the diagram 'Different types of feathers'.

Flight feathers These are found in the wings and tail. They are responsible for giving the bird uplift and stability in flight. Each flight feather is made up of a large, stiff and rigid rib or quill. The feather blade or vane is made of barbed feather strands that lock together. If these become separated, the bird can preen them back into position to reform the feather blade or vane again.

A variation of the flight feather is often found in the tail of the male as the showy sickle feathers and side hangers down each side of the true tail. The sickle feathers are probably seen at their largest in the Leghorn male in full feather.

Different types of feathers

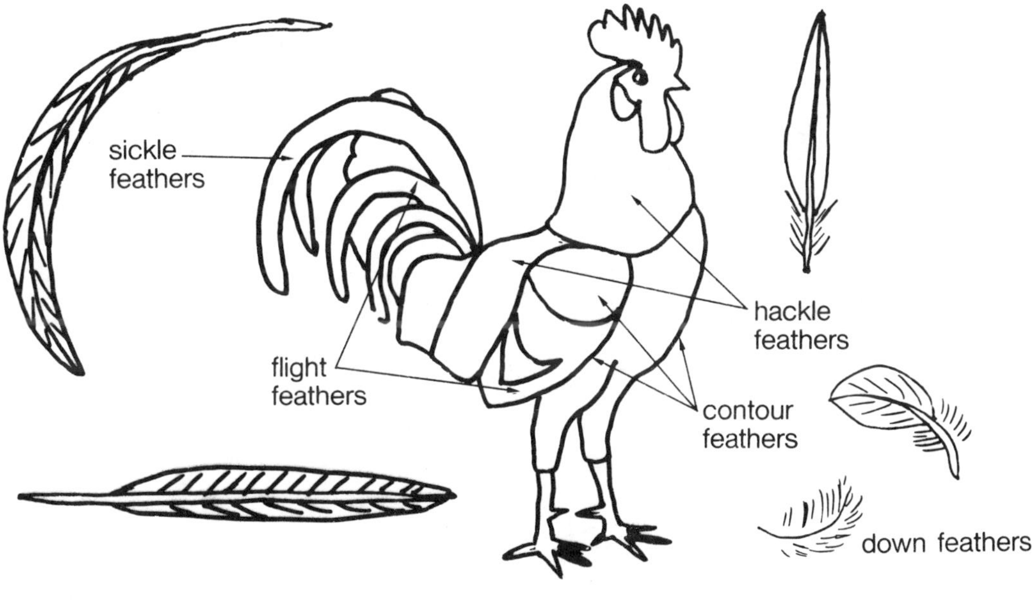

Contour or body shape feathers These feathers follow the line of the bird and give it its characteristic shape. Some follow the body contour more tightly than others as seen in the game fowls or more loosely as seen in the soft feather fowls e.g. the Orpington breeds.

This group of feathers are smaller than the flight feathers and consist of:

1. A small thin shaft
2. A small vane occupying the majority of the feather's length
3. A small amount of fluff adjacent to where the feather meets the skin.

The major types within this group are the covert and hackle feathers. In many breeds these feathers must be of a particular colour or pattern for a fowl to conform to a particular breed standard.

Down feathers These are located on the under surface of the fowl and around its vent. They are small, have a very thin shaft with feather strands that do not join together. These keep the fowl warm and are important when a hen is brooding a clutch of eggs.

Any discussion on fowls' feathers must also include talk of moulting. This is the annual loss and replacement of a fowl's feathers. It takes place in the autumn period and is related to a shortening of daylength. Refer to the diagram 'The biological clock and moulting'. During this period the hen goes off the lay. Large amounts of protein are needed to produce a new coat of feathers and as egg production also requires large amounts of protein, both processes cannot continue at the same time, so the fowl stops laying. Egg production also decreases in response to the shortening daylength of autumn.

Moulting can also be induced by drastic changes in diet, radical changes in weather patterns, external parasites or water shortage. Commercial egg producers induce moulting by dietary manipulation to speed laying hens through the moult as while they are not laying, they are not producing income.

Internal functioning of the fowl

As with all higher animals, the bird has a well developed skeleton performing the following functions:

1. Supports the body. It provides a frame on which

The biological clock and moulting

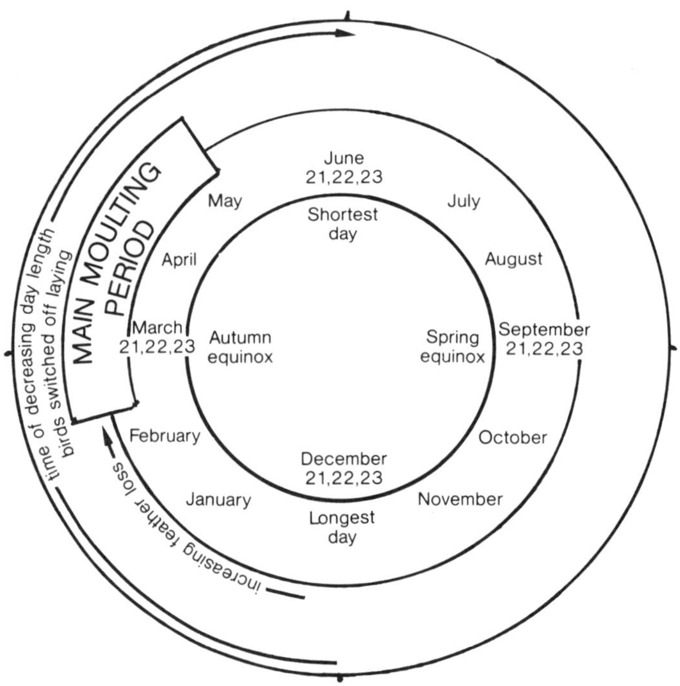

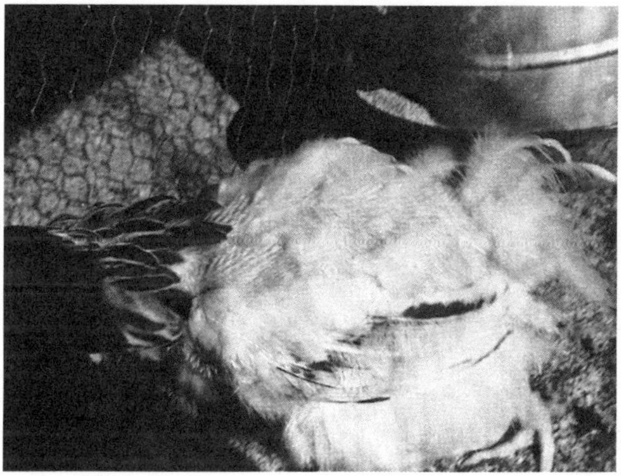

Sussex hen deep in moult. Back feathers have fallen out. New feathers can be seen appearing.

White Leghorn male well into autumn moult.

Old English Game blue red hen half moulted. Note new tail feather emerging.

Bantam hens well into moult.

other organs are supported, contributing to the bird's shape.

2. Protects vital organs such as the brain, heart and lungs.
3. Provides points of attachment for muscles.
4. Being jointed it allows the bird to move and fly.

There are two important differences in the fowl's skeleton when compared with that of other animals. Firstly the backbone is rigid. This provides a solid base against which the wing muscles can be contracted strongly when the bird is flying. Secondly, the interior of many of the large bones provides a storage of calcium that is needed for producing egg shells during the laying season.

How the fowl uses its food

The fowl obtains the nourishment it needs for its body by the process of digestion which takes place in the bird's digestive system. This system is shown in the diagram 'Digestive system of the fowl'. The basic function of the digestive system is to turn the large insoluble food molecules present in the bird's food into small soluble molecules (particles) that can be easily absorbed through the bird's intestinal wall into its blood stream.

Let's follow the passage of food eaten by a fowl. (See diagram 'Digestive system of a fowl'.)

The digestive system of the fowl

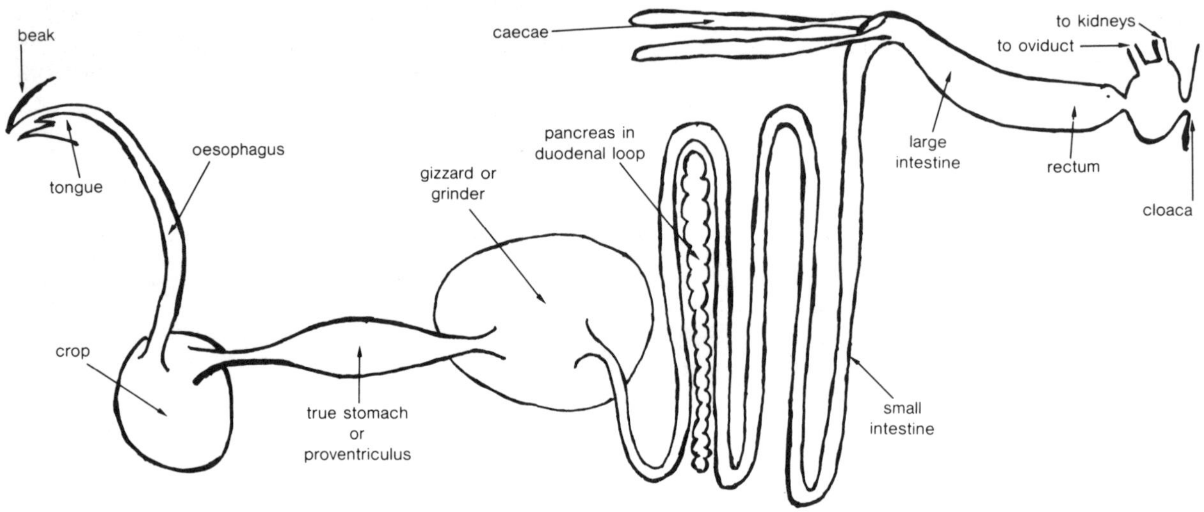

1. **Beak** This is used by the fowl for gathering the food it eats. Inside the mouth it is moistened by saliva to make it easier to swallow. This swallowing occurs by a natural reflex as the moistened food nears the back of the tongue.

2. **Oesophagus** This is a muscular tube that joins the back of the mouth and the crop. Waves of muscular movement (peristalsis) move the food along it and into the crop.

3. **Crop** A thin walled bag-like structure found near the front and base of the neck. It is quite prominent after the bird has eaten. This organ acts as a temporary storage for the food, which, during its stay, is softened by the moistening action of the saliva.

4. **Proventriculus** At this stage the food passes through the breast between the wishbone and into the true stomach or proventriculus. Here the food is treated with acidic gastric (stomach) juice that further softens it and starts the digestion of proteins.

5. **Gizzard** Since the fowl has no teeth with which to grind up its food, it is the gizzard ('grinder' or 'giblets') that performs this function. It is a muscular thick walled organ with a tough leathery inner surface. Whilst the fowl is foraging for food, it picks up stones and grit that remain mixed with the food in the gizzard. The combination of the gizzard's muscular movements, its leatherly surface and ingested grit breaks the food down to a fine state.

6. **Duodenal loop** When the food enters the duodenal loop it is treated with secretions from the pancreas located in the loop. There are two parts to the pancreatic juice:

(i) An acid neutralising juice to neutralise the acid effects of the gastric juice and

(ii) A solution of food splitting enzymes that break up the large food particles into smaller simpler ones that can be easily absorbed through the intestinal wall and into the blood stream. Examples of such reactions include:

(a) Proteins	Protease → enzyme	Amino acids
(b) Carbohydrates	Carbohydratease → enzyme	Glucose and other simple sugars
(c) Fats and oils	Lipase → enzyme	Fatty acids and glycerol

7. **Small intestine** The principal role of this organ is food absorption. Its structure permits a large absorbing surface to be contained in a relatively small volume: features include its long length, coiled shape and internal surface that contains projections called villi. The food is absorbed through these thin walls into the blood stream and transported to the liver where it is temporarily stored. The liver directs the food to the parts of the body where it is needed or changes some food into forms that the fowl may need, for example amino acids and proteins.

8. **Caecae** The remaining food material passes two blind tubes, the caecae, whose function is unclear. There is some suggestion that some food breakdown by microbe action may occur.

9. **Large intestine** This is not a particularly long organ in the fowl when compared with other animals. This organ serves as a water reabsorbing organ turning the undigested food into a semi solid mass.

10. **Rectum** The latter part of the large intestine where the unwanted and undigested food known as faeces is temporarily stored prior to voiding.

11. **Cloaca** This is a common opening in the bird for the digestive, urinary and genital systems. The kidney waste is added to the faeces at this stage and explains why fowl droppings have white patches on them.

The total process from beak to vent takes between 24 and 48 hours.

How a hen produces an egg

Increasing daylength and temperature in spring provide the stimuli that starts the hen laying. Let's trace the development of an egg in the hen. It is best to consider the egg's formation from the inside to the outside to understand the process. The major stages in an egg's formation are:

1. Yolk formation
2. Egg white formation
3. Membrane formation
4. Shell formation

1. **Yolk formation** This is the first stage of the egg's formation and takes place in the ovary where the female sex cell is surrounded by a large amount of fat and protein (yolk), and then by a yolk (viteline) membrane. The yolk is then released from the ovary into the funnel (infundibulum) of the oviduct where, if sperm are present, the egg will be fertilised. The chalazae (membranous twisted strings by which the yolk-bag is kept in position) are also added at this stage. The egg remains here for about 15 minutes before moving to the magnum section of the oviduct.

2. **White formation** In the next three hours as the yolk passes through the magnum, the egg white is placed around it.

3. **Membrane formation** During the following 1¼ hours, the two shell membranes, the inner and the outer, are formed around the yolk and white as they pass through the isthmus.

3. **Shell formation** By far the greatest amount of time, some 21 hours, is spent in the shell gland where the shell is formed around the membranes, white and yolk. The egg is now ready to lay, large end first tapering to the smaller end as it is expelled from the oviduct. When the egg is first laid, it is wet but as it dries the shell becomes characteristically brittle. This explains why the egg from a hen disturbed on the point of lay rarely breaks.

The total process takes between 25 to 26 hours and explains why a hen will lay progressively later each day. If an egg is due after about 4 o'clock E.S.T., it is held back and laid early the next day.

Once an egg has been laid, another yolk is usually discharged from the ovary about 30 minutes later to start the egg forming process again. This process is diagrammatically illustrated in the diagram 'The formation of a hen's egg'.

The formation of a hen's egg

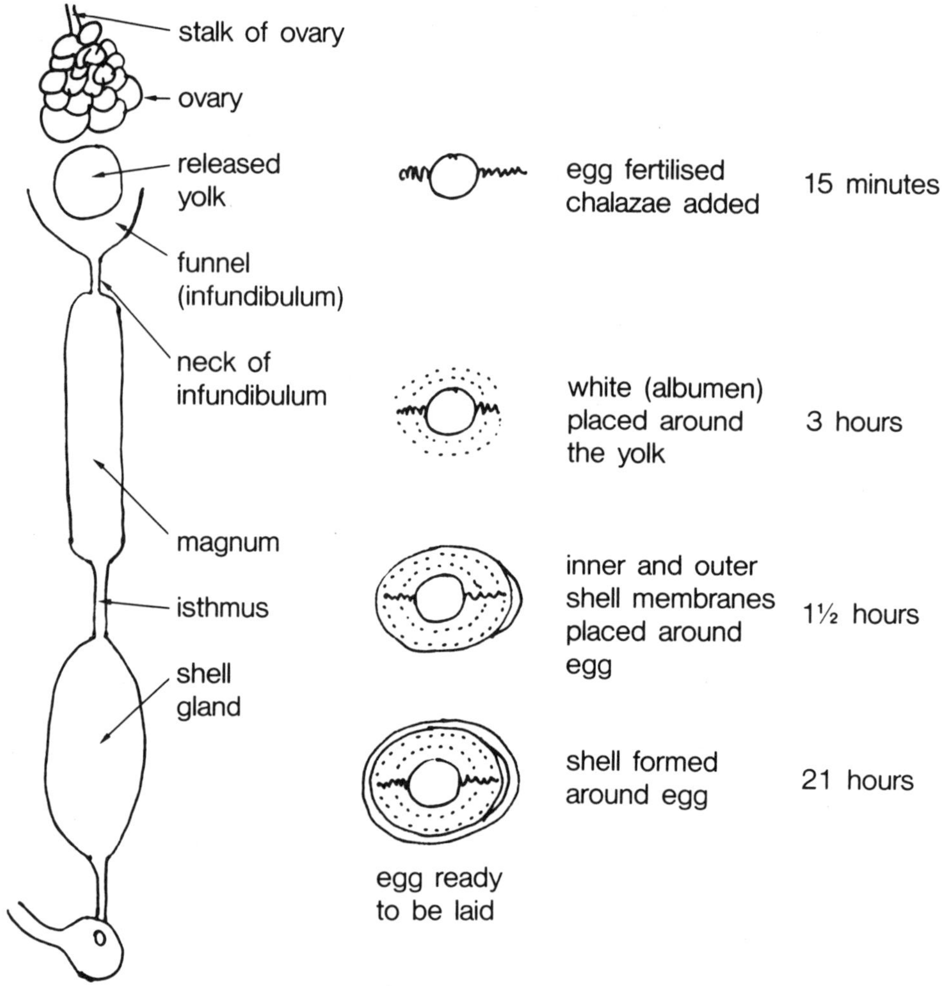

Major parts of an egg

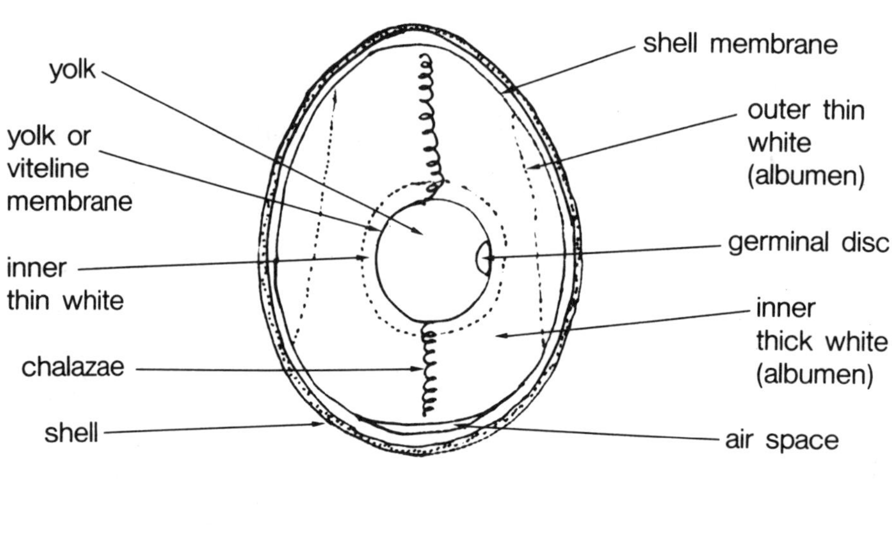

4 Poultry Nutrition

In the previous chapter, we have seen how the fowl absorbs the food particles it needs from its ingested food materials. This chapter deals with the fowl's nutritional needs and how it obtains them.

The fowl's nutritional needs can be placed into four categories:

1. Energy to maintain the processes we call 'life' as well as for movement, growth, body heat production and egg production.
2. The basic structural materials needed for growth and maintenance of the fowl's body. These are needed for bones, muscle, skin and feathers.
3. Substances that are involved in the correct functioning of the fowl's body. These include vitamins and minerals.
4. The nutrients needed for the production of eggs.

These needs are met by the fowl absorbing the following food groups from its ingested food during the process of digestion:

1. Water
2. Energy foods including carbohydrates, fats and oils
3. Proteins 4. Minerals 5. Vitamins

We shall now look at each of these food groups and see how they satisfy the nutritional needs outlined above.

1. Water

Some 50 to 60% of the fowl's body and 70% of the egg's contents consist of water. It is essential for the large number of chemical processes that occur in the fowl and a high quality supply must be readily available at all times. The sodium chloride (common salt) content must not exceed 4 500 parts per million. The need for water will vary between seasons. For example, 10 laying hens will need 4 litres of water per day in winter but will need 5 or more litres in summer. Particular attention has to be paid to the supply in summer as it has to be kept cool as well as clean.

2. Energy foods

Carbohydrates

This group is generally called the sugar group and is regarded as the major source of energy for the fowl. Sugars are made up of the elements carbon, hydrogen and oxygen with the ratio of hydrogen to oxygen always being 2:1. They are classified according to their complexity:

The **monosaccharides** Glucose is the most common example. This group can be directly used in the fowl's body functions. All other sugars must be broken down to these simple sugars before they can be used by the fowl. If they are not used immediately, they can be grouped together (condensed) to form sugars that can be stored.

The **disaccharides** These are split into two simple sugars (monosaccharides) which can be used as outlined above. Two common examples of disaccharides used in feeding poultry are malt sugar found in barley and lactose sugar found in milk products.

The **polysaccharides** are made up of many simple sugars condensed together. Starch is the most important example of this group in poultry nutrition. Starch is found in many cereal grains such as wheat, oats, barley, maize and sorghum. The fowl breaks down the starch into simple sugars (monosaccharides) which it uses as previously outlined. Another example of this group is cellulose. The simple sugars are so tightly condensed that the fowl is unable to digest cellulose down to its simple sugar components and it simply passes through the fowl's digestive tract as roughage. A small percentage of roughage (fibre) is necessary for the correct functioning of the digestive system.

Fats and oils

Fats and oils represent a concentrated store of energy: they supply 2¼ times the energy of a similar weight of carbohydrates. For this reason, they are included in commercial rations to boost the energy level of the food. This is particularly important in the broiler (meat chicken) industry where high energy levels are needed to support the rapid rate of growth of the broiler chicken.

Chemically, fats and oils are made up of the same elements as carbohydrates i.e. carbon, hydrogen and oxygen, but owing to their chemical structure, store much larger amounts of energy.

Fats and oils also supply important fatty acids that are used structurally in the fowl. Without these, chickens show slow growth and scaly skin conditions.

The yolk of the egg contains a high percentage of fat, some 32%, hence the need for a relatively high energy level in the food of laying hens.

3. Protein

Proteins are the basic structural material of many parts of the fowl's body including muscle (meat), nerves, skin, blood cells, feathers and eggs. In addition, the hormones and enzymes that control the chemical processes that take place in the fowl, are also made up of proteins. As a result, any shortage of protein below the fowl's basic requirements has a pronounced effect on its growth and production. In many cases, a fowl's poor growth or egg production can be traced back to a protein shortage.

Proteins themselves are made up of basic building blocks called amino acids. There are about 22 different types of amino acids present in protein. They could be compared to the letters in the alphabet that can be arranged in many different combinations to give us the words of our language. The 22 different types of amino acids are similarly used by the fowl's body to build up all the body structures. About half of the amino acids are regarded as essential, i.e. they must be present in the fowl's food, whilst the other half can be made from the essential amino acid group. Much of this process takes place in the fowl's liver.

4. Minerals

Current research shows that 16 minerals are essential for a fowl's growth and production. They may have a structural role or are involved in the fowl's metabolism (body's chemical processes). They are generally divided into two groups depending on the relative amounts needed by the fowl. The first group is required in relatively large amounts and are called major minerals. They are calcium, phosphorus, potassium, sodium, sulfur and magnesium. The second group is required in relatively small amounts but are none the less essential for the fowl's correct growth and production. This group includes iron, zinc, copper, manganese, iodine, cobalt, chlorine, molybdenum, selenium and fluorine. Some, such as fluorine, can lead to poisoning (toxicity) if they are over supplied.

Minerals of practical importance to the poultry fancier are:

Calcium, which is structurally important in bones and egg shells as well as being an important constituent of the fowl's body fluids. A calcium shortage results in weak bones, slow growth, poor shell quality, low production and poor hatchability.

Phosphorus, that is important in bone formation and shell quality. Phosphorus is structurally necessary in many important proteins as well as being part of substances important in respiration (the process by which the fowl derives energy from its food).

Potassium, with its role in the balance of the fowl's body fluids.

Sodium, which has an important influence on the fowl's body chemistry, egg size and the growth of chickens. Care must be taken not to over supply sodium in the fowl's diet.

Sulfur, as a key part of feather protein and egg yolks.

Magnesium, with its essential role in growth.

5. Vitamins

Vitamins are a group of substances that are required in very small amounts but are needed for the correct functioning of the fowl. Some are needed structurally whilst others are needed in the fowl's body processes. Around 20 vitamins have been identified but only 13 have been found to be necessary for poultry. The important ones are as follows:

Vitamin A, a shortage of which causes depressed growth, general weakness, low egg production and poor hatchability.

The B Group vitamins which are associated with respiration (energy release) and sugar use in the fowl's body. Some of this group are associated with fat and protein use.

Vitamin D which is associated with the fowl's use of the minerals calcium and phosphorus. A shortage of Vitamin D generally becomes a problem where fowls are housed out of direct sunlight.

Vitamin E and its importance in breeding stock. A shortage of this vitamin can result in reduced semen production in males, poor egg production in females and poor hatchability at incubation time.

Feeding fowls

Now that the fowl's nutritional needs have been outlined, what foods do they have to eat to meet these needs?

Carbohydrates These are generally supplied by using cereal grains e.g. wheat, maize, barley, sorghum and oats or cereal by-products.

Fats and Oils Normally supplied by oil seed meals, meat meal and tallow.

Proteins Common protein rich foods (concentrates) include lucerne meal, soyabean meal, blood meal, fish meal, meat meal and grain pollard.

Minerals Ground limestone, bone meal, shell grit, blood meal and specific minerals salts.

Vitamins These are supplied in green feed, grains or synthetic additives.

To correctly feed fowls all their nutritional needs means providing a wide range of foods. As well, it must be remembered that when fowls are 'free ranging' there is no guarantee that their full nutritional needs will be met. This presents a strong case for basing the feeding of fowls on a commercially prepared food.

If all the abovementioned foods were simply mixed together the fowl would pick and choose just as we do at a smorgasbord, paying little attention to our proper nutritional requirements. To

Typical poultry feed labels

1

15% GROWER CRUMBLES

MEDICATED WITH A COCCIDIOSTAT

ANALYSIS

Min. Crude Protein	15.0%
Max. Crude Fibre	6.0%
Actual Crude Fat	7.0%
Actual Salt	0.5%
Max. Fluorine	.035%
Max. Urea	Nil

NET WEIGHT 45 kg

081261

2

INGREDIENTS

Wheat, Barley, Sorghum, Oats, Lucerne Meal, Soya Bean Meal, Cotton Seed Meal, Meat & Bone Meal, Blood Meal, Rice Pollard, Salt.

Vitamins AD3, E, K, B1, B2, B6, B12, C, Niacin, Cal Panto, Choline Chloride, Copper, Iron, Zinc, Manganese, Iodine, Biotin, Methionine, Butylated Hydroxy Toluene, [illegible]coban.

3

16% LAYERS MASH

(Registered Under Stockfoods and Medicines Act, 1940)

INGREDIENTS

Wheat, Barley, Sorghum, Meat and Bone Meal, Soyabean Meal, Lucerne Meal, Rice Pollard, Ground Calcium Carbonate, Methionine, Potassium and Manganese Sulphate, Zinc Oxide, Vitamins A, D3, E, B2, B12, K, Niacin, Calcium Pantothenate, Choline Chloride and Butylated Hydroxy Toluene.

CHEMICAL ANALYSIS

Min. Crude Protein	16%
Actual Crude Fat	4%
Crude Fibre Max.	9%
Actual Salt	1%

NET WEIGHT WHEN PACKED 45 kg

004414

Label 2 is the reverse of label 1. It shows the ingredients needed to formulate the grower ration. Label 3 shows the ingredients used to formulate layer mash or crumbles.

Inspection of the analysis will show differences in the formulations.

overcome this, commercial poultry feed is pelletised or made into crumbles so that, as the bird eats, it picks up particles which supply all of its nutritional needs. This further strengthens the case for using commercially prepared feed.

Modern poultry nutrition has now reached the stage of computers being used to formulate poultry rations. Because large feed companies are able to buy large quantities of feed at one time, they are able to purchase their food materials much cheaper than the poultry fancier. Mixing his own feed would therefore prove more expensive per bag than commercially purchased feed.

It is the feed bill that is the biggest expense in poultry raising. The poultry fancier must decide how much he is prepared to pay out annually on feed before he decides how many fowls he wishes to keep. It is false economy to try and save on feed when the result is a group of malnourished, disease prone, poor growing and poor performing fowls.

The following figures will give some idea of the amount of food consumed by different classes of large fowls. It would be fair to assume that bantams would eat about 25% to 33% of the figures given below. These figures are for an average sized growing pullet from day old to point of lay:

0– 4 weeks	0.5 kg
5– 8 weeks	1.2 kg
9–12 weeks	2.0 kg
13–16 weeks	2.5 kg
17–20 weeks	2.9 kg
	9.1 kg

It must be remembered that many factors could change these figures upwards such as weather conditions, quality of housing and breed. Heavy breeds e.g. Sussex and Australorp would consume more feed.

Once fowls reach maturity, it can be expected that they will consume around 4 kg per month.

Using these figures, it would be reasonable to assume that the average large fowl would consume around 52 kg of feed per year or a little over one 50 kg bag.

Now returning to the point raised about how much a fancier is prepared to pay for food each year. It can be seen that keeping each fowl is an expensive investment. The expense, however, can be used as motivation for careful and continuous culling of fowls that fail to reach a required standard, as well as motivating careful breeding and selection. One could ask 'Is that fowl worth a bag of feed over the next 12 months?'

In summary, once a fancier has established how much he is prepared to pay out for feed each year, the selection of the type of food should be based on a commercially formulated mixture to avoid potential nutritional problems.

5 Common Pests and Diseases of Poultry

Any other organism that lives on, in or frequently visits the body of the fowl, from which it obtains food, may be termed a *pest*. These irritate the fowl, make it loose its appetite, or in sufficient numbers, and this is generally rare, may cause it to die. These pests are often termed *fowl parasites*.

On the other hand, a disease results from the upsetting of the normal healthy state of the fowl. This can result from a number of causes:

1. A response to an invasion by a large number of parasites.
2. Invasion by infective agents (pathogens) such as bacteria, protozoans, viruses and fungi.
3. Nutritional deficiencies caused by poor feeding and watering.
4. Stress caused by poor housing, leading to overcrowding, chilling or overheating.
5. Poisonous substances that have been misplaced by careless use.

It is the purpose of this chapter to deal with the major infective agents and their resulting diseases. Points (3) and (4) should not be a problem with proper attention to feeding and housing. Point (5) should not be a problem if proper care is taken with the use of agricultural chemicals in and around the fowl yard. It is the legal duty of all people using agricultural and garden chemicals to be familiar with the chemical being used by reading and understanding the labels on the container. The label's precautions and safety directions must be strictly adhered to. If in doubt check with your chemical supplier, Department of Agriculture or vet.

Common pests or parasites of fowls

These are generally divided into:

1. Internal parasites, which are those that live inside the fowl's body,

and

2. External parasites, that live on or visit the outside of the fowl's body.

Internal parasites

Worms are regarded as the major group of internal parasites that infest fowls. These worms cannot be passed on to humans, so there is no danger to the poultry keeper. The important worms infesting fowls are:

a) Large Round Worms
b) Caecal Worms
c) Tapeworms
d) Capillaria
e) Gizzard Worms

The most common sites of worm infestation are shown on the diagram 'Common worms in fowls'. Of these, the Large Round Worm is the most common and the one most likely to be found in a poultry fancier's yard. Caecal worms are believed to be a carrier (vector) of Blackhead disease and this presents a good reason for not running domestic poultry and turkeys together, turkeys being very susceptible to this disease. Tapeworms are more likely to occur where fowls are running free as the tapeworm needs intermediate hosts such as earthworms, snails, flies or beetles to complete its life cycle. Capillaria and Gizzard worms are lesser problems to the poultry fancier.

Since the Large Round Worm is the most important and common of the fowl worms, we shall look more closely at its effects on the fowl, life cycle and control. The most common signs (symptoms) of an infestation are general weakness, loss of appetite, drooping wings, ruffled feathers, diarrhoea and yellow or blood stained droppings.

How is the Large Round Worm controlled? Control is aimed at attacking the worm at a number of points in its life cycle. The more places the life cycle can be broken the better the chance of success in controlling this worm. The usual control measures are as follows:

1. Maintenance of a proper diet, as well fed fowls are more resistant to worm infestation.

Common worms in fowls

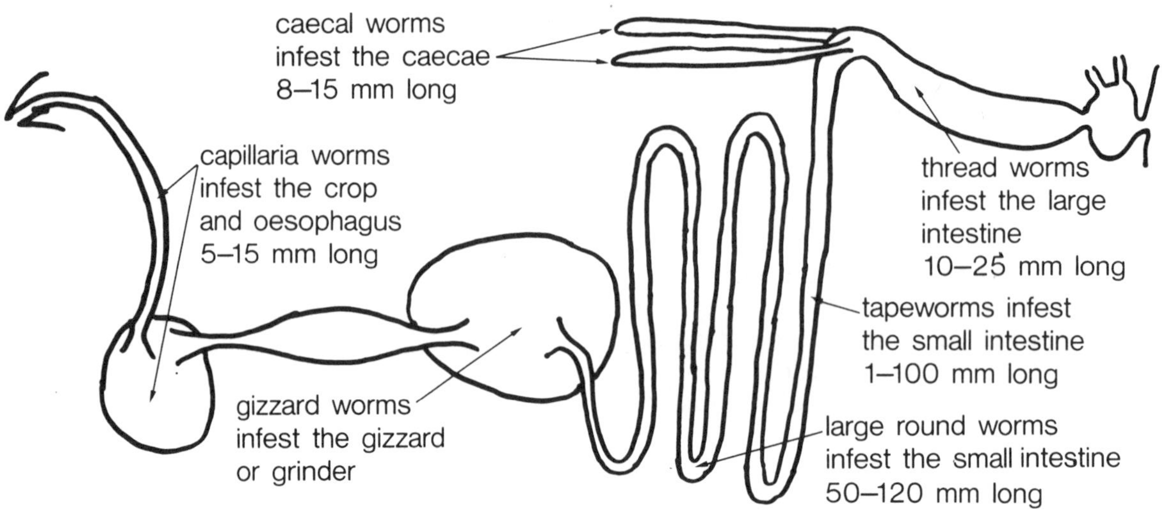

Large round worm life cycle

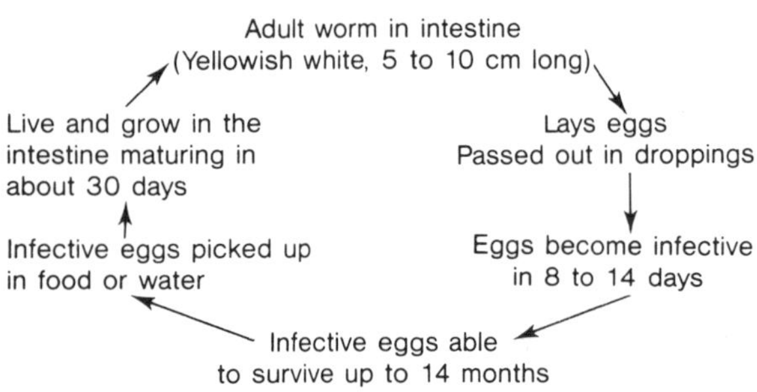

2. Sensible management practices such as not running young and old fowls together, avoiding overcrowding, not allowing an excessive build up of manure, and not running fowls on damp litter or in wet yards.

3. Medication by way of a routine worming program using chemicals such as Piperazine and Levamisole (Nilverm®). The most convenient method of administration is to remove the drinking containers on the evening prior to worming and give the fowls medicated water (chemical in the drinking water) next day when their thirst will ensure that they drink. The chemical manufacturer's instructions must be read, understood and strictly adhered to. If the above mentioned strategy is followed worms will not be a problem.

Drinking water worming method. The normal automatic waterer is raised some time before worming water is introduced, making the fowls naturally thirsty. When the worming water is introduced the fowls will readily drink the medicated water. The drink container is stabilised with half a brick.

External pests or parasites of fowls

This group consists of those organisms that live on or visit the fowl's body.

Lice

Lice are wingless, grey or amber coloured insects about 1–3 mm long that spend their entire life cycle on the fowl. There are a number of types of lice taking their names from thc part of thc fowl whcrc they are most likely to be found, for example body louse, shaft louse (shaft of feathers), wing louse and fluff louse. They are spread from one fowl to another by physical contact and it is often the male in a breeding pen that is most heavily infested with them. Fowl lice will not survive on humans as their diet is made up of fowl skin fragments and debris; there is no danger to humans handling a lousy fowl. Fowls with heavy lice infestations suffer weight loss, lower egg production and feather damage caused by the constant irritation of the lice on their skins. Lice are most likely to be a problem during the autumn–winter period.

The louse life cycle is brief and rapid with an adult pair of lice producing up to 100 000 off-spring in three to four months.

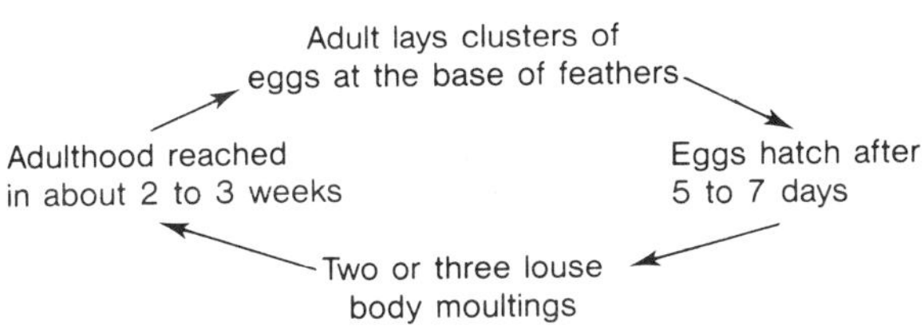

Birds naturally reduce lice numbers by regular dust bathing so it is advisable to provide some dry, sheltered dust bathing conditions for fowls. Where this cannot be provided chemical control measures will be necessary and the following methods can be used:

1. Where numbers are small, dusting the individual fowl with insecticide dust is practical. During dusting, each bird can be individually checked for lice.
2. Spraying fowl sheds with an approved insecticidal solution such as Malathion or Carbaryl. Food and drink containers must be removed and the manufacturer's instructions followed.

Two external parasites of fowls

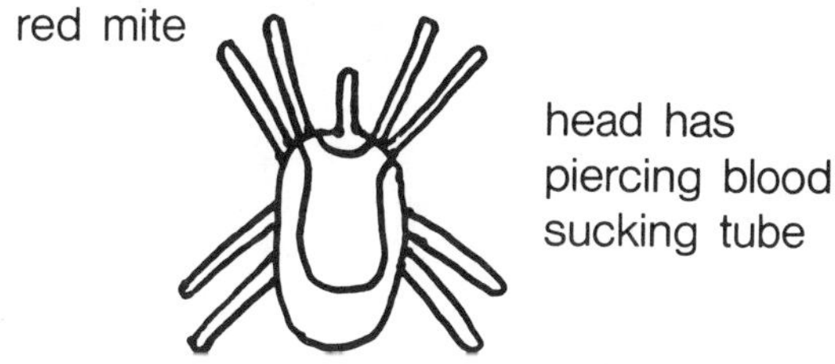

size: just visible to the naked eye

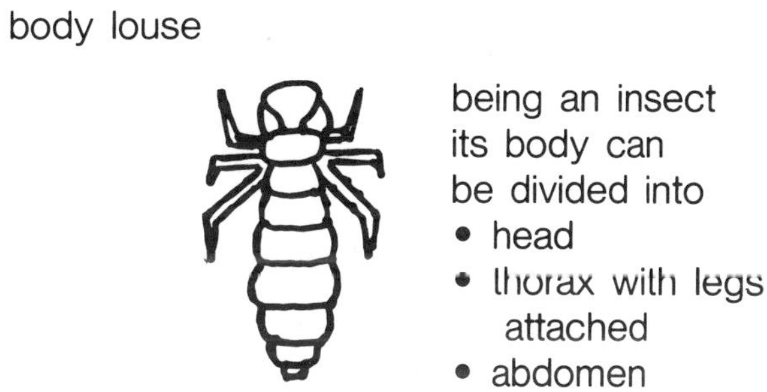

size: 1 to 3 mm long

Mites

These are smaller than lice and are only just visible to the naked eye. The two mites of concern to the poultry fancier are the red mite and scaly leg mite.

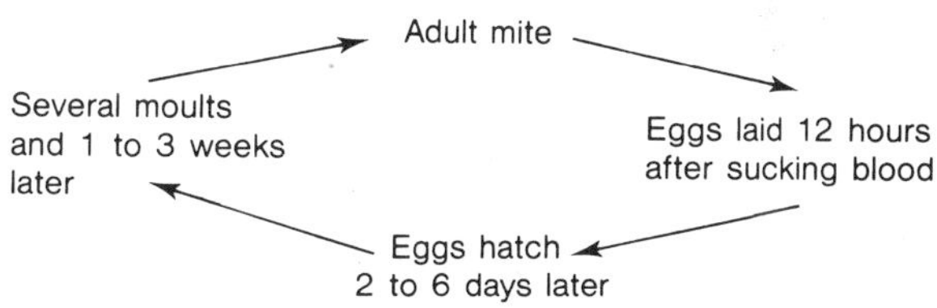

Red Mite This is a blood sucking mite that feeds at night, preferring to hide away during the day in cracks and crevices inside the fowl shed. Since it sucks blood, it has been linked with the spread of Fowl Tick Fiver and possibly Leucosis. It also has a simple life cycle. Control measures involve spraying the fowl house with approved insecticide solutions each 3 to 4 weeks until the red mite is controlled. They are best seen by visiting the fowl house at night with a torch. The mites will scurry away when disturbed by the torch light.

Scaly Leg Mite Once again, a very small creature that spends its life cycle on the fowl. Its presence is noticed by the outward turning scales on the bird's shanks. If left unchecked the legs become enlarged and take on a grotesque appearance. It is associated with older fowls. The condition is caused by the mite irritating the flesh at the base of the scale. The mite's very location makes it difficult to control. Traditionally, sump oil or a mixture of sump oil and kerosene were painted onto the legs to control the mite. However, most poultry fanciers scrub the legs with warm soapy water to soften the scales, then apply petroleum jelly sometimes mixed with sulfur, or an oil for example baby oil or olive oil. When dusting for lice, some of the powder will fall on the legs and shanks also affording some control.

Fowl Tick These are more a problem west of the Great Divide. The tick is large, being up to 10 mm long and ranges from amber to purplish blue in colour depending on whether it has had a meal of blood. They are nocturnal feeders so a visit with the torch at night can also act as a check for these. During the day, like the Red Mite, they hide in cracks and crevices around the fowl shed. Being a blood sucker, they produce poor growth, lowered production and anaemia. They are carriers (vectors) of Fowl Tick Fever (which will be discussed in the section on diseases). Ticks are difficult to control, with the main method being to spray the fowl shed with an approved insecticidal solution.

Stickfast Flea This pest attacks the head, comb, eyes, earlobes and wattles where it attaches firmly to the skin, hence its name. Since the poultry fancier is keen to maintain the heads of his fowls in top condition, a check must be made for these pests. Fortunately, it seems to be limited to western NSW at this stage. Lice dusting powder helps control this pest.

Mosquitoes During wet summers, mosquito numbers can increase to such a level that they can greatly irritate fowls, mostly at night time. They are known to be vectors (carriers) of Fowl Pox. A spraying program using an approved insecticide can reduce numbers during times of heavy infestation.

Some common chemicals used to control poultry parasites. Left to right: *Dibrom® for mosquito control, Fowl and Fowl House Spray, Maldison® for external parasites, Nilverm® for worm control.*

Common infective agents and their resulting diseases

Viruses

Marek's Disease

This disease does not become apparent until the fowl is about 14 to 16 weeks of age when birds develop lameness, drooping wings or leg paralysis, as one form of this disease attacks the nerves of the fowl, especially in the legs. Another form of the disease causes tumours (cancers) in the vital organs, ending in the death of the bird.

The best method of avoiding the disease is to vaccinate day old chickens as they leave the incubator. Once vaccinated, they must be kept well isolated from older fowls for fourteen days while they develop immunity.

One disadvantage of using broody hens for hatching chickens is that they can be introduced to the Marek's disease virus directly from the broody hen and, since they need fourteen days in isolation to build up resistance to the Marek's disease organism, there is little use in vaccinating such chickens against the disease.

The vaccination involves injecting vaccine subcutaneously (under the skin) in the back of the neck (see accompanying photograph).

Fowl Pox

This appears as wart like growths on the comb, wattles and breast of the fowl. To the fancier it is important because if an infected fowl recovers, the wattles and comb are often disfigured. Fowl Pox is most likely to be a problem in late summer and autumn when mosquito numbers are often at their highest.

Fowl Pox is usually controlled by a wing stab vaccination. See accompanying photograph. This is generally given when the chickens are 7 to 10 days of age and again at about 12 weeks of age. It is an advantage to also vaccinate adult fowls in December.

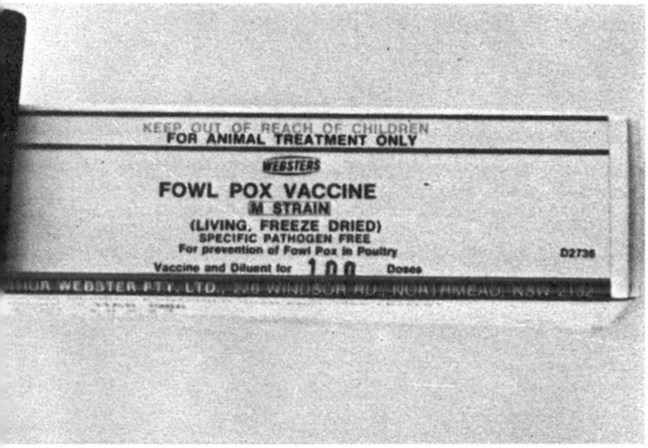

Fowl pox vaccine and special double pronged needle used to give young fowls a wing stab vaccination.

Two other viral diseases that can be prevented by vaccination are:

Infectious Laryngeal Tracheitis (I.L.T.) which is an acute infammation of the windpipe (trachea) which eventually causes obstruction of the respiratory system.

Infectious Bronchitis (I.B.) which is also a respiratory disease but mainly of chickens and young adults. Both diseases can be vaccinated against by giving the vaccine as an eyedrop.

Protozoans

The major protozoan disease of fowls is **coccidiosis**, which caused high mortality amongst chickens and young fowls until the introduction of commercially prepared medicated food. The idea is to give the young fowls some protection against coccidiosis while they build up resistance to the organism. This is why chicken crumbles and grower food is labelled 'medicated with a coccidiostat'. The coccidiostat does not completely kill the coccidia (disease causing organism) but reduces its effect to such a level that the fowl's body can build up a resistance. The disease can also be treated by using chemicals such as Sulfaquinoxaline in the drinking water. The coccidia life cycle is summarised below

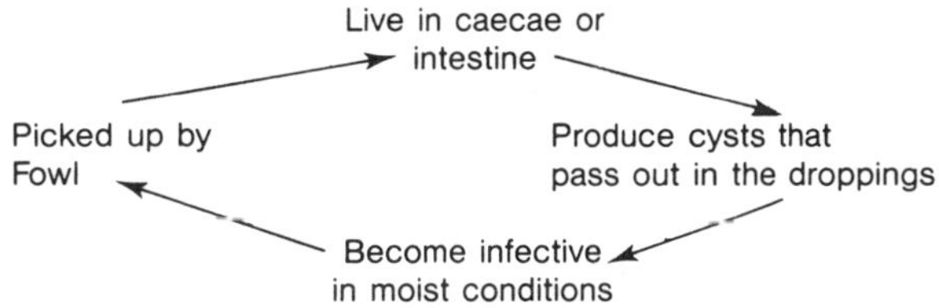

In chickens, the symptoms are depressed appetite, ruffled feathers, watery droppings, often with blood, and sudden death. The usual method of control is mainly preventive, involving keeping chickens and young fowls dry, feeding commercially prepared crumbles containing a coccidiostat, and avoiding running young stock and old stock in the same pen.

Bacteria

Three bacterial diseases affecting poultry are:

Pullorum which the State Department of Agriculture's testing program has reduced the incidence of.

Chronic Respiratory Disease Where outbreaks occur they are treated with antibiotics and can be lessened by sound management as well as correct housing.

Coryza The fowl appears to have a 'cold' with a watery, bubbly discharge from the nostrils, and can be treated with antibiotics.

Fowl Tick Fever

Caused by a microbe passed from one fowl to the next by blood sucking parasites such as Fowl Tick, Red Mite and mosquitoes. The fowl may die suddenly or become depressed, pass greenish diarrhoea, go lame in the wings or legs and die in convulsions. Control is by vaccination at 12 weeks of age with a repeat dose given four weeks later. A booster dose should be given each 12 months to adult stock.

Vaccination

As can be seen from the foregoing, management plays an important role in preventing disease.

However, it is advisable to combine sound poultry management with a vaccination program. This becomes even more important when the poultry fancier takes his fowls to poultry shows. It is better to have the fowls protected against disease where possible rather than have a fowl catch a disease at a show and bring it back to infect your fowls at home. Further, it is a pity to put so much effort and time into breeding and preparing a top fowl only to lose it from a disease that could have been prevented. The following is an example of a vaccination program:

day old — Marek's disease
1 week — Fowl Pox—wing stab
4 weeks — Infectious Bronchitis—eye drop
8 weeks — Infectious Laryngeal Tracheitis—eye drop
12 weeks — Fowl Pox—wing stab
Fowl Tick Fever
16 weeks — Fowl Tick Fever

An automatic, adjustable inoculator (vaccinator) is a worthwhile investment that speeds up vaccination. They are available from vaccine suppliers.

It is important to read, understand and follow the manufacturer's instructions on the storage, mixing and preparation of the vaccine. One area of particular importance is that vaccines should not be exposed to heat or sunlight. A small six pack foam cooler with a layer of ice inside makes an ideal storage for vaccine whilst needling fowls. Always try to vaccinate in the shade. It is better for you, the birds and the vaccine.

There are good reasons for vaccinating on a co-operative basis:

1. Two or three people make vaccination quicker. Two catchers come holders and one vaccinator.
2. If the people involved synchronise their hatchings, large enough batches of chickens can be assembled to match up with the minimum vaccine pack sizes, usually 100 doses, thus saving money.
3. There is less likelihood of a vaccination being put off with the pressure from others acting as a reminder.
4. Provides a good social get together to talk about up and coming hopefuls.

In summary, pests and diseases should not be a problem if you manage your fowls well, that is

Subcutaneous (under the skin) vaccination in the skin at the back of the head as used on day-old chicks for Marek's disease vaccination.

Eyedrop vaccination used to vaccinate against infectious laryngeal tracheitis (I.L.T.).

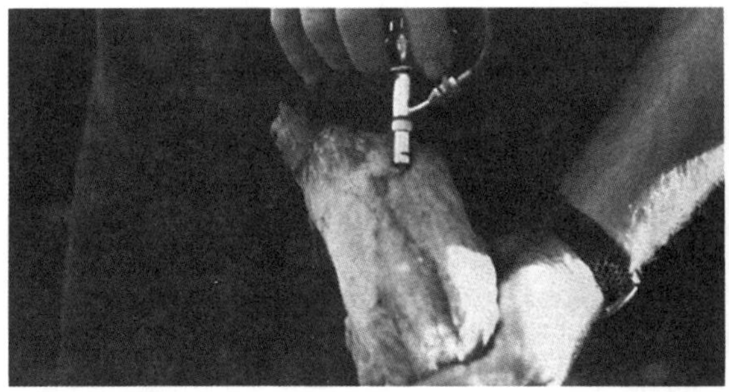

Intra-muscular injection into the breast muscle parallel to the breastbone that is used in the fowl tick fever vaccination. The thigh muscle is an alternative site for this injection.

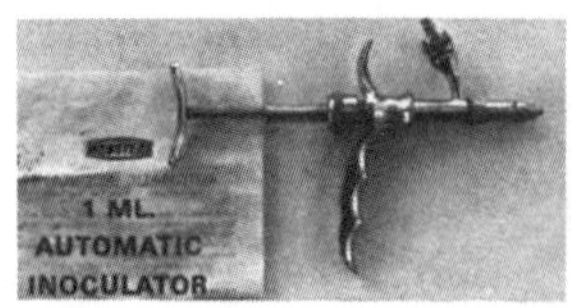

(Left) *1 ml automatic inoculator* (right) *Automatic inoculator connected to vaccine on ice in foam cooler.*

- feed them well
- house them properly
- regularly inspect them
- worm them regularly
- dust them and spray their quarters with a suitable insecticide
- have a vaccination program
- show care with agricultural or garden chemicals near or around the fowl yard.

6 Housing Poultry in the Backyard and on the Hobby Farm

Before specifically looking at individual housing facilities, let's outline what poultry housing should provide.

1. protection from the extremes of weather
2. protection from predators such as foxes and dogs
3. a place to roost or camp at night
4. feeding and watering facilities
5. laying facilities for laying stock.

There are many forms of poultry housing ranging from the intensive set up of the commercial producer, to the semi-intensive housing of the backyarder through to the free range system of many rural areas. All cater in varying degrees for the above mentioned points. The following is an outline of the three basic systems of poultry housing.

Commercial housing

This system is aimed at satisfying purely commercial goals such as:

1. consistency of supply
2. sustaining a high quality of product
3. a low unit cost of production
4. maximising output
5. obtaining high food conversion to products
6. minimising labour input.

For this reason, two different types of commercial housing have been involved.

1. the intensive cage system for laying hens where many thousands of hens are housed in specially designed cages. These cages are enclosed in a shed designed to cope with the extremes of climate.
2. the intensive deep litter sheds used for the production of broilers (meat chickens), where the chickens are run on a deep litter of shavings, sawdust or rice hulls.

Whilst poultry fanciers' goals are different, much of the technology from the intensive poultry industry can and has been adapted to their systems of housing. These will be mentioned as they are encountered in this chapter. We can now turn our attention to the systems normally used by the poultry fancier.

Semi intensive housing

Basically, this includes fowls that are housed in sheds on deep litter or fowls that have a roosting shed and a yard to restrict their movement. Typical semi intensive shed setups are shown in diagrams 1 and 2.

The positioning of the shed is very important; it should have a north easterly aspect allowing the sun to shine in the front of it, particularly in winter when the sun is at a much lower angle to the ground. A correctly positioned shed will allow the winter sun to warm the fowls but shade them in the summer. See diagram 3.

Free range system

This system is restricted to farming locations for reasons that will become apparent. It simply provides a place for the fowls to roost at night. At one extreme, they may simply roost in trees or farm sheds and on the other, they may have a fowl house into which they are locked at night following the evening feeding. As the name implies the fowls spend the day ranging around scratching and feeding. Whilst the fowls may be given grain or crumbles in the evening, much of their food is obtained during the daily scratching and ranging. Whilst this natural system of fowl raising is relatively cheap to set up and has many advocates, it does have its draw backs, such as:

1. fowls prone to be taken by predators.
2. difficult to find eggs which are also often dirty.

Semi-intensive housing

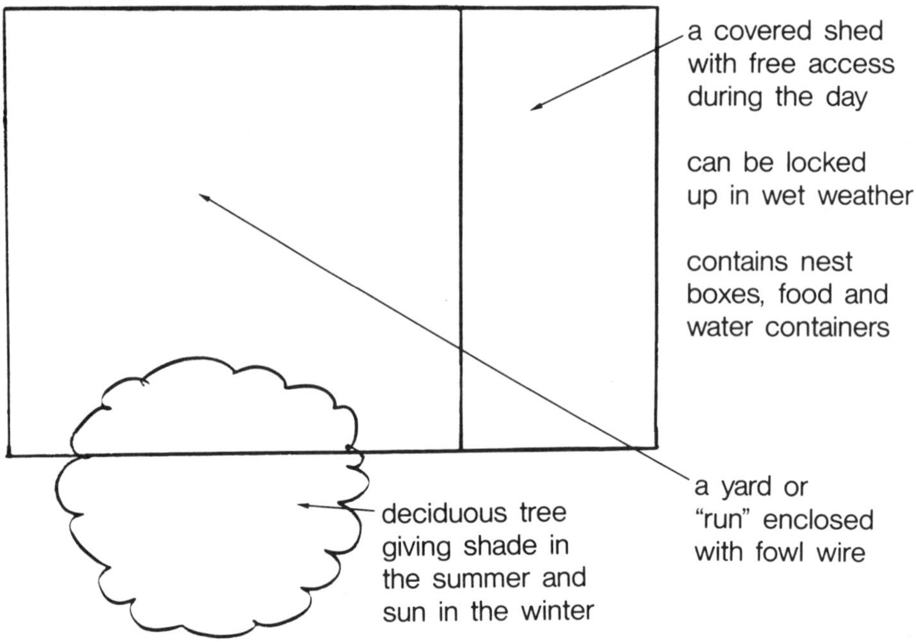

Semi-intensive shed

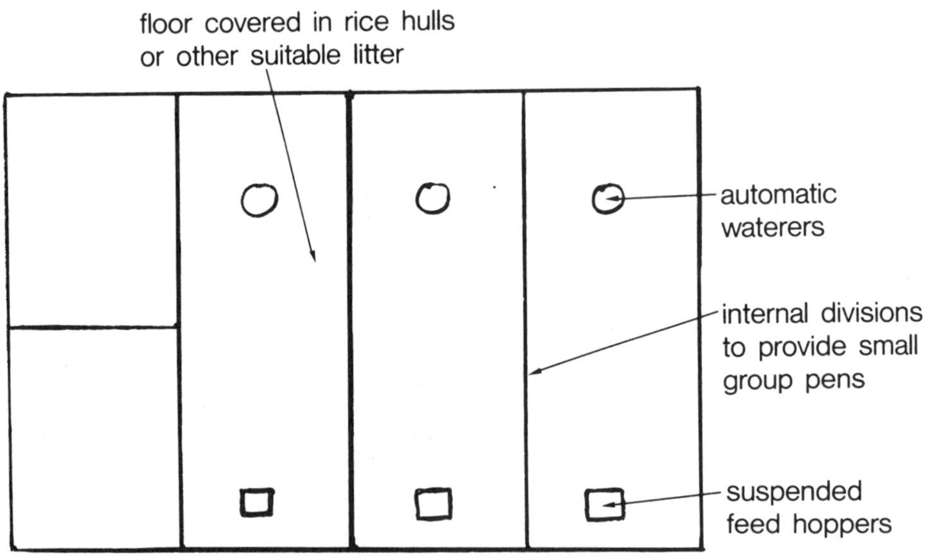

3. harder to keep an eye on the fowls and manage them.
4. greater chance of contracting tapeworms as part of the fowls' diet will be made up of the intermediate tapeworm hosts, for example beetles, snails and earthworms.
5. harder to monitor their diet to ensure their nutritional needs are met.
6. older and younger birds running together complicates disease control, for example coccidiosis and worms.
7. sun bleaching of plumage, an important consideration with coloured exhibition poultry.

Fowls from a well managed free range system do, however, show excellent body condition resulting from the exercise of running around.

The angle of the sun

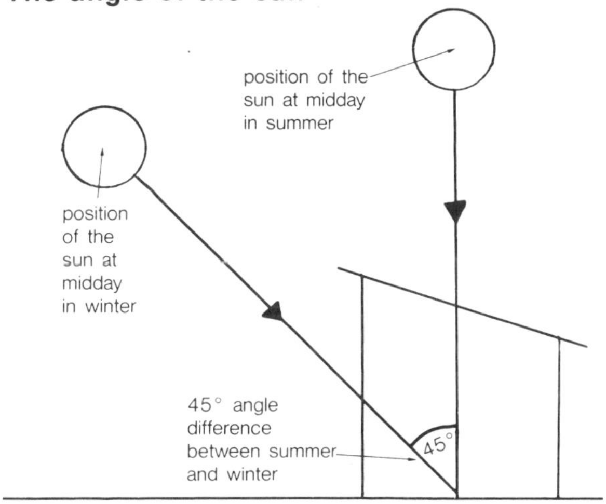

Shows the difference in the angle of the sun between summer and winter. With the shed positioned with a north easterly aspect, the winter sun will warm the fowls during the cold weather but they will be shaded during summer.

The system of housing to be chosen will depend upon personal choice, location and how much a person is prepared to pay out for materials. One important aspect is to make sure that you comply with your local Council's regulations on the keeping of poultry, so check with them first.

Housing exhibition poultry

We shall now look at two housing systems that have been used to house poultry and cope with the specific needs of exhibition poultry. Before doing so, we will list the important basic needs that have to be met. They are facilities for the following:

1. show training 2. breeding 3. brooding 4. growing.

One problem that is faced by people starting off breeding and exhibiting poultry is that they tend to focus only on the fowls they take to the show. However, to ensure they have a show team the following season, they have to provide for the other three requirements of breeding, brooding and growing. This consideration is often neglected by beginners who obtain more breeds than they can conveniently manage. Far more success and satisfaction is achieved by concentrating on one or two favourite breeds and providing proper housing for them. This results in a smaller, more compact and easier to manage set up which the fancier can effectively run, rather than the hobby running him. Whilst there are many devoted poultry fanciers who spend many hours with their fowls, and enjoy it, those new to the fancy would be best to start in a small way so that the fowls do not become a burdensome chore interfering with their other interests. It gives time to decide the level of involvement. Many successful fanciers have emerged by simply concentrating on one breed or variety and doing it well.

We shall now look at two set ups that have been used by two successful breeders and see how they have handled these housing needs.

The first is that used at a high school in NSW. It is basically a semi intensive shed system. (See diagram.)

How does the system cope with the housing needs outlined?

High School semi-intensive shed. Show training pens on far left side. Open sides for plenty of ventilation. Side walls to 1 metre to afford fowls protection at litter level.

High School semi-intensive shed. Automatic drinker used to maintain a good quality water supply.

The high school system

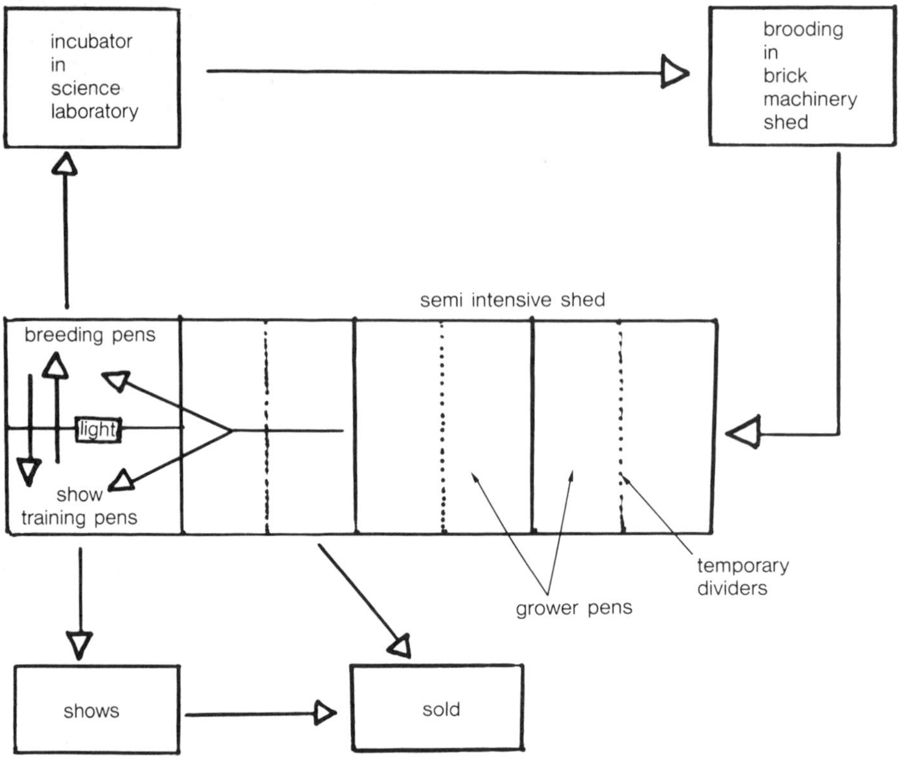

1. **Show training facilities** are pens housed inside one end of the shed. The shed is equipped with a light so that the fowls can be trained at night when they are more responsive. The light also assists with the catching of fowls when taking them to shows and re-penning upon return from shows. Mostly this is done before sunrise and after sunset so a light makes the job much easier.
2. **Breeding facilities** are housed in the same part of the shed as the show training pens. Sometimes show fowls are mated whilst being part of the show team so it is convenient to have the fowls closely housed adjacent to the show training pens. Eggs from the breeding pens are hatched in isolation in the incubator located off the farm in the school's science laboratory.
3. **Brooding facilities** Once the chickens are hatched and vaccinated for Marek's Disease, as outlined in the chapter on pests and diseases, they are brooded in isolation in a brick machinery shed. Here they stay until 6 weeks of age.
4. **Growing facilities** At this stage, the chickens are shifted to the semi intensive shed where they are placed in grower pens that have been previously

Food supplied by hoppers. Note garbage bin used as a bulk feed store adjacent to the hopper. Australorp cockerel.

Young Light Sussex growers separated into sexes by a temporary pen divider.

White Leghorns on deep litter. Closed side to 1 metre to afford fowls protection, but the open side allows good ventilation.

depopulated for several months, sprayed with an approved insecticide and have a new litter of rice hulls placed on the floor. The grower pens are divided up by temporary dividers to suit the needs

Breeding pen facilities. Breeding trio of White Leghorns.

of the growers at the time, and each pen has its own automatic waterer and feed hopper. These are ideas borrowed from the intensive commercial industry. As soon as the pullets (females) and cockerels (males) can be distinguished, they are separated into like groups. Here they remain until they become part of the show team, breeders or are sold.

The second system is one used by a successful young breeder to raise bantams. (See diagram.)

Once again, we can see that the four major requirements have been met.

1. **Show training facilities** are housed in the backyard poultry shed. The cage fronts are similar to those used in a show pen so the fowls are familiar with their surroundings on show day.

A backyard system for raising bantams

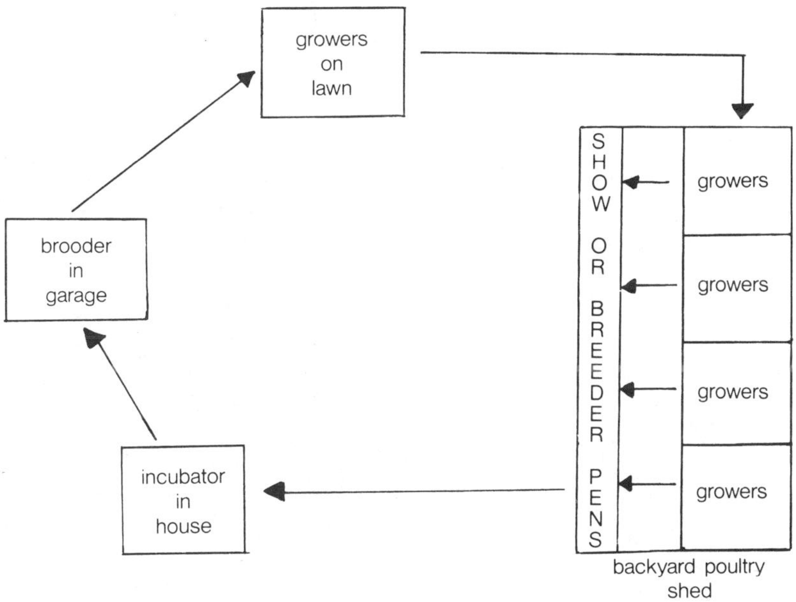

Backyard poultry shed. Sheet galvanised iron is used to afford protection against winds. Shade cloth is used to shade fowls but still permit adequate ventilation. The general floor area is raised above surrounding level and has a deep layer of litter on it.

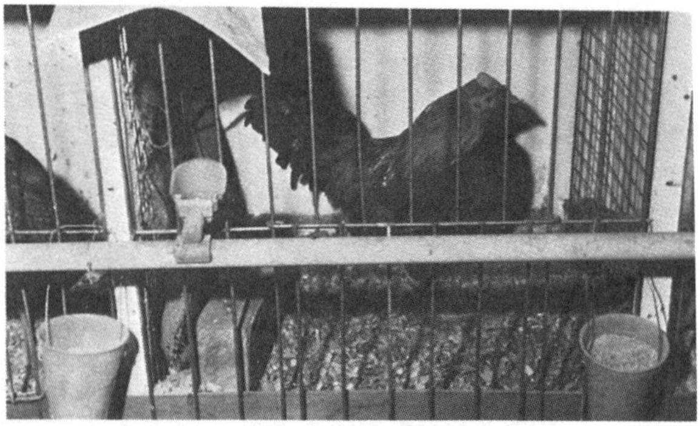

Close-up of a show training pen that can also double as a breeding pen for a breeding pair.

Show training facilities

A breeding pen suitable for a breeding pair or trio.

Grower pen of males run on deep litter, with an automatic waterer and food hopper in the background.

A group of growers in a grower pen.

A group of female growers in a deep litter pen.

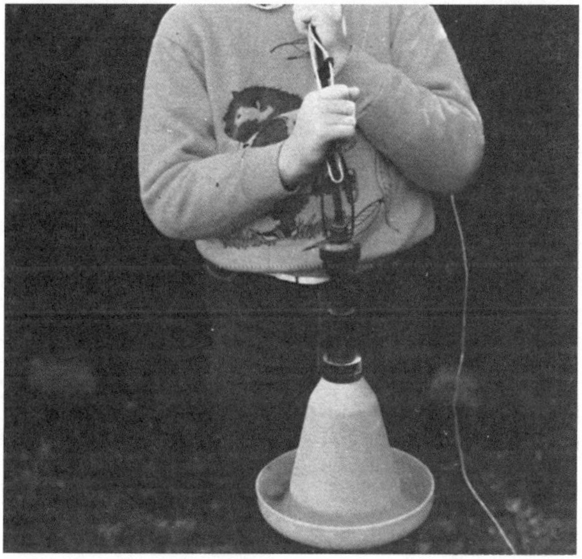

Automatic waterer used in a backyard poultry shed.

Portable grower pens suitable for running groups of 10–12 bantam growers on the back lawn.

2. **Breeder facilities** Since breeding involves using specially selected pairs, the show training cages double as breeder cages. The eggs from the breeding pairs are transferred to the incubator located in the house during the breeding season.
3. **Brooding facilities** consist of a temporary brooder that is set up in the garage, giving the chickens the isolation necesary for building up resistance to Marek's Disease. These are vaccinated at day old as they leave the incubator and are transferred to the brooding facilities.
4. **Growing facilities** This system consists of two separate parts. Firstly, small wire mesh cages are used to house the young growers from the brooder on the back lawn. Secondly at 12 to 16 weeks, they are transferred to the grower yards in the main poultry shed. These grower yards have been previously emptied at the beginning of the breeding season to allow at least four months depopulation as a disease prevention measure. Growers that are not retained as part of the show team or breeding team are sold prior to or by the breeding season.

In summary, when housing poultry, the following should be remembered:
Firstly, be aware of your local Council's regulations concerning poultry before you start.
Secondly, your choice of housing should be such that the following things have been provided for:

1. protection against the extremes of climate
2. protection against predators
3. a safe place to roost or camp at night
4. provision of feeding and watering facilities
5. provision of laying facilities for laying stock.

Thirdly, in most cases a variation of the semi-intensive system of housing would best suit the needs of the average poultry fancier.

7 Breeding Fowls

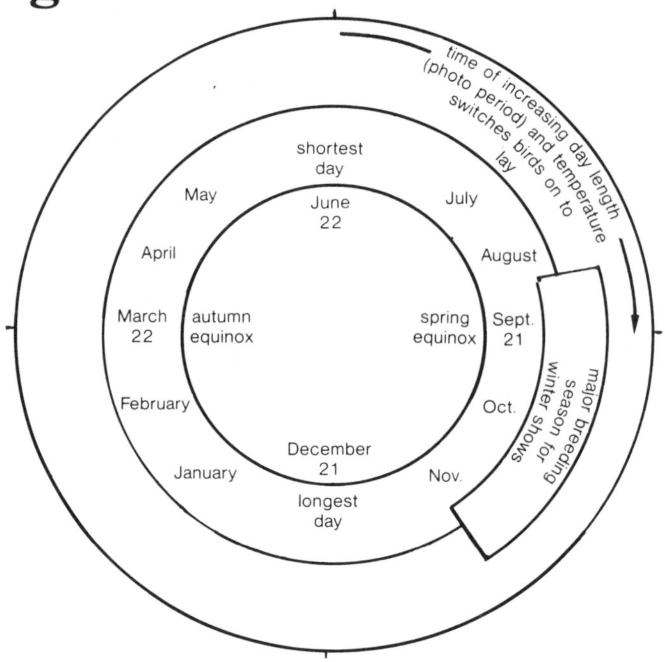

The biological clock and the breeding of birds

Day length

Before discussing the breeding of fowls in detail, it is relevant to consider the influence of day length and temperature on the natural breeding habit of birds. Birds will start to breed when they have warm, gradually increasing temperatures and experience increasing day length (photoperiod). These stimuli act on the bird's pituitary gland in its brain which in turn triggers the release of the hormones responsible for controlling reproduction. Such conditions are experienced in spring and this is the reason why we see birds nesting at that time of the year. This idea is illustrated in the diagram 'The biological clock and the breeding of birds'.

Fowls raised under natural conditions also follow this pattern and it is spring that is regarded as the major breeding season for pure bred poultry. A knowledge of the fowl's response to day length is made use of commercially to overcome shortages of eggs in the late autumn–winter period. Laying fowls are subjected to an increasing photoperiod made up of the natural daylight and an amount of artificial light which would give the birds light conditions similar to that experienced in spring. As a result, the birds continue to lay when they would normally have ceased laying.

If we look at a poultry fancier's calender, we find that the majority of specialist poultry club shows are held over the May–June–July period each year. This is just prior to the normal breeding season. By using the natural spring breeding season, the birds are between eight and twelve months of age at the next show season.

The reproductive systems

The basic egg laying system of the female has already been discussed in an earlier chapter. It would be useful to return to that section and review how an egg is formed. For a fertile egg to be produced, the female must have been mated (been 'trodden') by a fertile adult male. The male stands on the female's back, whilst flapping his wings for balance, and brings his vent (cloaca) into direct contact with the female's vent. Sperms (male sex cells) are passed from the rooster into the female's oviduct. The sperms then swim along the mucous

The reproductive system in birds

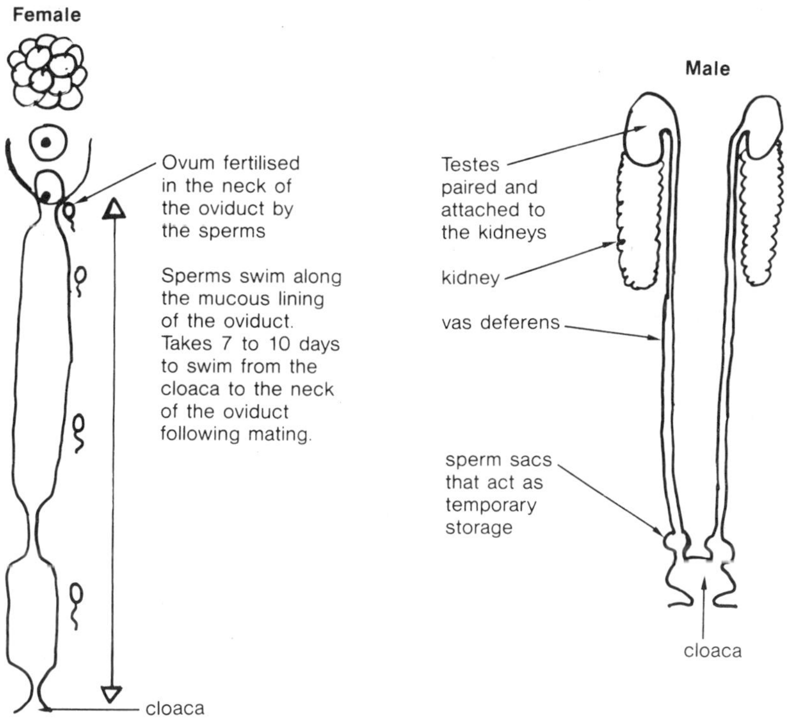

covered lining of the oviduct until they reach the neck of the oviduct (infundibulum) near the ovary. Here the sperms can fertilise the ovum (female sex cell) as it passes attached to the yolk into the oviduct in the egg forming process. It takes a period of time for the sperm to swim from the cloaca to the neck of the oviduct and this is why it is some seven to ten days after mating before fertile eggs can be expected. Likewise, a hen can continue to produce fertile eggs for up to seven to ten days after mating.

The male has a pair of testes attached to the kidneys located close to the back of the bird. These produce the sperm which passes down a tube called the vas deferens to a small sac adjacent to the cloaca. These sacs serve as a temporary storage of sperm prior to mating. Both reproductive systems are shown the diagram 'The reproductive system in birds'.

Breeding pens

With a view to producing offspring with desired features, fanciers spend much time selecting their fowls for mating and arranging them as 'breeding pens'. A breeding pen may consist of a rooster and a single female (a breeding pair) or a rooster and two females (a breeding trio) or a rooster with any number of females up to twelve (a breeding pen). The number of females a rooster can be mated to in a breeding pen situation ranges from eight with heavy breeds such as Australorps and Sussex to twelve with the light breeds such as Leghorns and Anconas. Which of the three systems is chosen will depend on how closely the breeder wishes to follow his matings. More on this later.

Before putting the breeding groups together, a number of points must be remembered.

1. Breeding stock must be well fed. The male needs a high level of nutrition to be active and produce viable sperm. For the female to produce top quality eggs, all her essential nutritional needs must be met. This is why many breeders use special high protein breeder rations to feed their breeding stock. At least a good quality (high protein) layer ration must be supplied, ideally supplemented with fresh green feed such as lucerne, spinach (silver beet) or clover.
2. The rooster's spurs should be trimmed with a

hacksaw to about 2 cm of the shank. If the bird is firmly held and a fine bladed hacksaw slowly drawn across the spur, little pain or bleeding will be experienced. This operation prevents the spurs cutting the sides of the female during mating, a problem which is accentuated when the birds are mated as pairs.
3. Some breeds have fluffy vents that must be trimmed to ensure that the male and female vents can join together without obstruction during mating. The vent fluff should be trimmed away with a pair of scissors.
4. The age of the fowl plays an important part in the breeding program. Whilst many breeders will not use pullets (females in their first laying season), there is no reason why they cannot be used if they are fully grown, are laying good sized eggs and are well fed, as pullets lay more eggs than hens (females after their first laying season). As a hen ages she lays between 25–30% less eggs per season and starts laying later each successive spring. However a breeder may tolerate this if the hen is a proven breeder.
5. In general, hard feather fowls, particularly the males, seem to have a longer breeding life than the soft feather breeds that are rarely kept for more than three breeding seasons.
6. Fowls of different ages can be used in a breeding program. For example, cockerels (first year males) can be used with hens, or cock birds (males after the first year) used with pullets. However, it is not advisable to place hens and pullets together with a male in a confined breeding group.
7. Apart from the seven to ten days needed before fertile eggs are laid, it is a good idea to have the breeding group together some time before the breeding season to allow the group to establish its social order. Introducing a new member to an established group means that the social order has to be re-established. This upheaval can throw a breeding female off the lay in some cases and thus delay the breeding program.
8. It is a good idea to leg band each of the breeding fowls so they can be easily identified later when young stock has grown. Numbered coloured plastic leg bands are available for this purpose.

Examples of nest boxes made from black plastic drums. A generous lining of wood shavings is provided for the hen to lay clean eggs on.

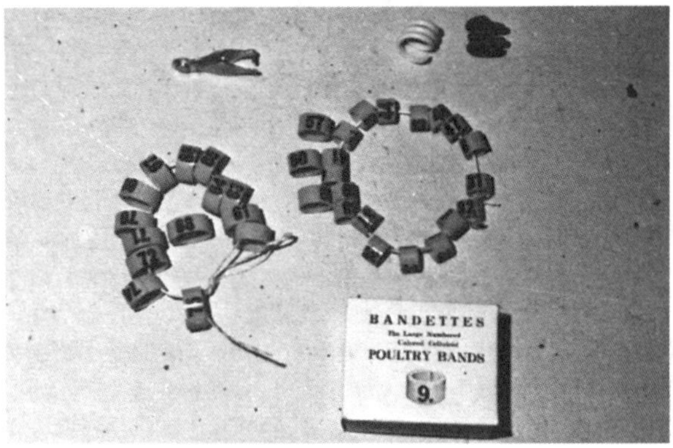

Poultry identification gear. Top left: *web or toe punch.* Top right: *spiral leg bands.* Lower left and right: *numbered plastic leg bands.*

Collection and storage of eggs for hatching

Now that we have assembled our breeding groups, we need to look at the important area of collecting and storing eggs suitable for incubation either under a broody hen (natural) or in an incubator. Nest boxes need to be provided. These should provide a dark clean place to lay eggs away from the general walking area of the fowls. They may consist of fruit boxes (wooden or cardboard), drums with one end removed, black plastic drums (see accompanying photo) or a sheet of material (metal, wood, fibro) leaning up against the side of the pen. Importantly, they should be lined with plenty of clean litter such as straw, shavings or rice hulls upon which the hens can lay clean eggs.

The eggs required for incubation should be collected at least once a day and have the date as well as breed written on the shell. Should the eggs be dirty, do not wash them but allow them to dry and brush them as clean as possible with dry steel wool. Eggs that have been washed clean in water tend to run a greater risk of decomposing and exploding ('bangers') in the incubator with smelly consequences. Any eggs' that are misshapen, cracked, undersized for breed, or have a spotty appearance should not be kept for incubation.

If eggs have to be stored, they can be kept in clean egg cartons point down. The cartons need to be kept in a cool place (not the refrigerator), free of draughts and wide temperature differences. Eggs are best set for incubation within a week, but can be stored in cartons for up to two weeks before drastic reductions in fertility are experienced, provided the carton is carefully turned over each day.

Breeding records

At this stage, it should become apparent that where there is more than one breeding group used for a particular breed, accurate records need to be kept. Unless a breeder knows the results of his matings, he cannot repeat his successes or avoid past mistakes. Such records should be able to identify:

1. The eggs from the breeding pen
2. The chickens that hatch from the eggs
3. The adult fowls that have grown from those chickens.

This is usually achieved by giving each mating a code or 'I.D.' that can be written on the eggs as they are collected from the breeding pens. On the final candling (checking the eggs' fertility) prior to placing the eggs in the hatching tray, eggs of a similar code can be grouped together in a separate hatching tray compartment. Once the chickens have hatched and fluffed up, they are given a toe (web) punch assigned to that breeding pen code on the egg. Toe (web) punching involves the removal of a small circular piece of the webbing skin found between the toes. If this is done correctly, the fowl will have a permanent round hole in its foot webbing for life. This means that a fowl can be traced back to the breeding pen. If you look at the diagram 'Toe punch markings', sixteen different

Toe punch markings

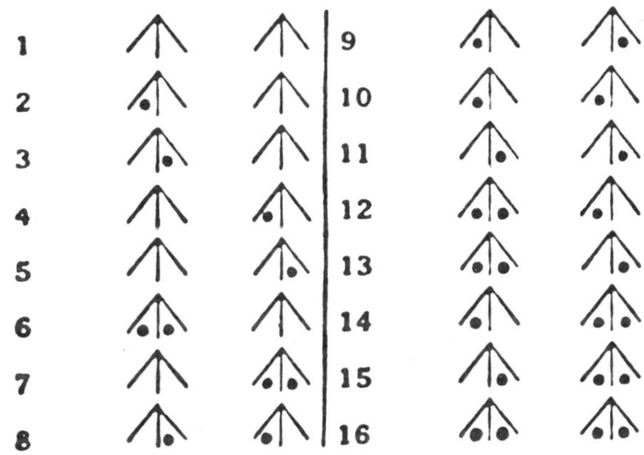

combinations are given which would be more than sufficient for most fanciers.

At twelve months of age, prior to the breeding season, the now adult fowls used for breeding are given a numbered, coloured leg band so that the series of toe punches can be used once again for the next season's matings.

An example is shown of a breeding record which attempts to satisfy all the needs mentioned previously and so allow the breeder to trace where his good birds came from, as well as locate any faults that may have arisen in the breeding season's chickens.

Breeding strategies

Single mating

As the name implies, a male is mated with a single female. This can be achieved by placing a male and female in a pen as a breeding pair, or where a number of females are housed separately and the male introduced either for mating only, or to spend a day with one female before being moved to the next. Under this system it is a good idea to have the male housed so that he can see the females to be mated so that he will readily tread a female once the two are placed together. This system also proves popular where a breeder still wishes to show a breeding fowl during the spring agricultural show season. Females left single mated without the male being removed will soon have the back feathers broken and damaged to such an extent that they are unsuitable for exhibition.

An additional benefit of this system is that fertility is almost ensured because you see the fowls mate. The male is given a one to one chance to mate, whereas in the pen situation he is more likely to mate with the more submissive females and be put off by the more bossy types.

Line breeding

Line breeding involves mating very closely related birds such as a rooster to his pullets (daughters or granddaughters) or a hen to her cockerels (sons or grandsons). Line breeding is undertaken with the aim of concentrating as many desirable features as possible in the resulting offspring. Coupled with a heavy culling program (removing unwanted types), the level of genetic variation is diminished with the hopeful outcome being highly desirable offspring of uniform type and quality. Certain lines of fowls have been developed this way without new introductions of unrelated fowls (outcrossing) being made for between 20 and 30 years. However, because line breeding involves mating closely related fowls, undesirable features such as low hatchability, poor fertility, low vigour, low disease resistance and decrease in size can result. The Anderson's Line breeding chart shows how a line of fowls can be developed from two carefully selected parents. It also shows the relative amounts of each parents' blood the offspring carries. Some breeders spend years developing lines of a particular breed (sometimes called 'strains'), and guard them so jealously that they are prepared to kill and eat surplus birds rather than let them fall into the hands of other people who may in turn set up parallel lines or strains.

Double mating

This breeding strategy involves the use of one breeding pen to produce exhibition males, and another to breed exhibition females. The practice is most commonly used for breeding Leghorns, particularly the coloured varieties such as the Brown and the Black. Unfortunately, with double mating, there is a large wastage of fowls, unless they are purchased by people familiar with the breed and keen to include such birds in their own double mating programs.

The Leghorn provides a good example of the use of double mating strategies. The discussion has been limited to the head and tail to illustrate the ideas behind double mating.

A mating to breed exhibition females The breeding female here should have an evenly serrated, single folded comb with a thin tail carried at 45° to the back. Such a bird should also be free of excessive saddle feathers around the base of the tail feathers. This is sometimes termed the 'cush'. The female breeding male has an evenly serrated clearly cut comb that is thin at the base causing it to gently curve over to one side. The tail should be thin and free from 'furnishings' (saddle feathers) around the base of the tail and have sickle feathers that are as poorly developed as possible.

A mating to breed exhibition males The male

Breeding record

Breeding pen 1		Chicken toe punch	Eggs set						Hatching tray						Chickens hatched						Chickens reared		Comments, e.g. cull %, problems
Male I.D.	Female I.D.		Date	Date	Date	Date	Date	Date	Date	Date	Date	Date	Date	Date	Date	Date	Date	Date	Date	Date	M	F	

How to line breed

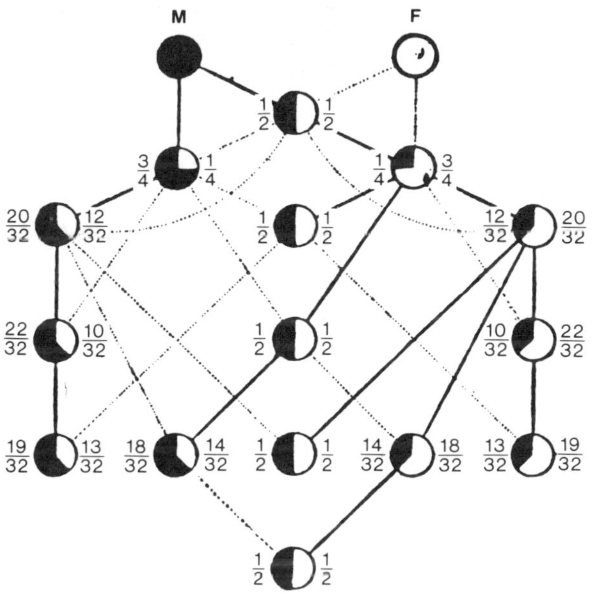

The accompanying illustration of what is known as Anderson's line-breeding chart shows that a son may be mated to mother and father to daughters, and how subsequent matings may be made. The black circle represents the male, and the white the female. The chart is read from the top downwards commencing with an unrelated male and female. These mated together produce progeny generally recognised as half blood of each parent. In subsequent matings as outlined on the chart, each solid line represents the male side of the mating and the dotted lines the female. The proportion of male to female blood in the resultant progeny of each mating is indicated by the amount of black and white in each circle. The most essential point in line-breeding is never to breed from any fowl with any defect or evidence of ill-health. It should be remembered that each individual inherits all the characters, both good and bad, of the race, thus the danger of any system of inbreeding of which line-breeding is a modified form, is apparent. The probability of reproducing or intensifying undesirable characters is lessened, however, if the cardinal principle of selecting breeding stock on the basis of stamina is rightly observed.

should have an erect, evenly serrated comb thick at the base to support it. The tail should be large with long flowing sickle feathers and well developed saddle hackle feathers around its base ('furnishings'). The female required to mate with this male should have an evenly serrated erect comb, a fan tail and well developed feathering around the tail base, i.e. a well developed 'cush'.

Whilst the female from the male breeding pen and the male from the female breeding pen are no use as exhibition fowls, and, to the uninitiated, would not appear to be very attractive or particularly useful, they are most useful as breeding fowls in the situation described above.

Compensatory mating

This could also be described as 'balanced mating'. A bird with an excess of a particular feature is mated to another with a deficiency of that same feature, in the hope that there will be an averaging or balancing effect. This is used in the Light Sussex breed where the amount of white bordering the neck hackle becomes too large giving the bird a 'washed out' appearance. Such a bird would be mated to a female with heavy black colouring running through the white border of the feather. The resulting offspring have a dark centre to the hackle feather with a thinner but complete white border.

Artificial Insemination

A further breeding technique that has been basically a poultry research technique is artificial insemination or A.I. It involves the collection of semen from a male and its transfer to selected females. This technique requires a level of technical expertise only achieved with practise, but has a number of benefits going for it.

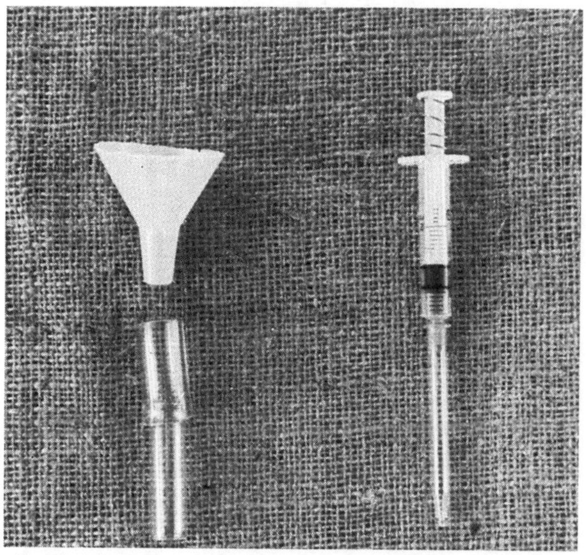

Artificial insemination equipment. Top left: *collecting funnel.* Bottom left: *collecting tube.* Right: *inseminator used to transfer semen from collecting tube to the female's oviduct.*

1. With careful dilution, up to ten hens can be inseminated with one semen collection, so the influence of a desirable male can be spread over a much larger number of females than under natural mating.
2. Females can be used for breeding whilst being shown, especially breeds such as the Pekin which would need to have their tails cropped in the breeding pen.
3. A male can be used for breeding whilst still being kept in top exhibition condition which is a fatter state than good normal breeding condition.

The accompanying photograph shows the major pieces of equipment needed to carry out this technique. However, most poultry fanciers prefer to use natural methods of breeding fowls and the use of A.I. is restricted to the enthusiastic specialist breeder.

It is probably beneficial for the beginner to be aware of any special breeding techniques needed by a favoured breed and decide whether he is prepared to adopt these before actually purchasing stock. It is probably far easier to select a breed where exhibition fowls can be bred from a single breeding pen, before endulging in those breeds that require double or compensatory mating. A good breeding pair or trio from a recognised breeder is the best start even though the initial outlay may be high. Good stock cost no more to feed than poor stock and since the food bill will be the most expensive item in looking after your fowls, there is little point in trying to eocnomise on cheaper breeding stock. The answer is buy the best available from a recognised breeder and be prepared to pay for it.

8 Incubation, Brooding and Raising of Chickens

This is probably the most fascinating aspect of raising pure breed poultry. The previous chapter dealt with obtaining fertile eggs from the breeding pen. We shall now follow the progress of the fertile egg from the time it starts its development to the time the resulting chicken has reached adulthood or in the case of the female, the time she starts to lay.

Incubation

The development of the single celled zygote resulting from the union of the sperm cell and the ovum at fertilisation into a hatched, fully developed chicken takes 19 to 20 days for true bantams and 21 days for large fowls. For this development to take place, three conditions must be met:

1. A constant femperature of 37–38°C.
2. A high level of humidity that prevents the drying of the eggs as the shell is porous and will allow moisture to escape from inside.
3. Regular turning for the first 18 days to prevent the developing chick sticking to the shell membrane. This occurs because the yolk floats upwards in the egg white and will press against the membrane without regular turning.

These conditions are met naturally by the broody or sitting female; if these three conditions can be met artificially, then fertile eggs will also develop chickens. As pointed out earlier, man has been successfully incubating fertile eggs for many thousands of years, since the days of the ancient Chinese and Egyptians. More recently, in a novel attempt to sell electric fry pans when they were first introduced into Australia, many electrical stores used an electrical fry pan with fertile eggs supported on a cake rack over water to hatch the eggs as a publicity gimmick. Of course, the eggs had to be painstakingly turned several times a day during the process. This exercise is not recommended for anybody interested in hatching their own fertile eggs but does show that fertile eggs can be hatched as long as the right conditions are provided.

An example of an electrically heated fan forced hobby incubator.

Incubators

The most common incubator used by the poultry fancier is a variation of the electrically heated, fan forced ventilation concept. These work as follows:

1. The eggs are placed in racks that can be moved either automatically or manually to facilitate egg turning on a regular basis.
2. The heat source is usually either a carbon filament lamp or a heating coil that is linked to a very precise thermostat. This switches the heat source

Incubator door open to show setting tray in incubating position. When the external lever is moved to face the opposite direction the setting trays will be tilted in the opposite direction. The eggs are turned through 90°. Hatching tray visible at the bottom of the incubator.

on and off to keep the interior of the incubator in the 37–38°C temperature range. Maintenance of this narrow temperature range is critical to the development of the chick.

3. The heat source is located over a container of water, so as the air is warmed a certain amount of water is evaporated to maintain a high moisture level (humidity).

4. A fan constantly mixes the air, keeping it at a uniform temperature. The diagram 'How an incubator works' illustrates the concept of an electrically heated, fan forced ventilation incubator.

Before using an incubator, it is essential that you are familiar with the operating instructions supplied with it. The machine must be set running at the desired temperature and humidity for at least 24 hours before placing any fertile eggs in it for incubation. Where a carbon filament lamp is used, it is advisable to have a spare lamp on hand.

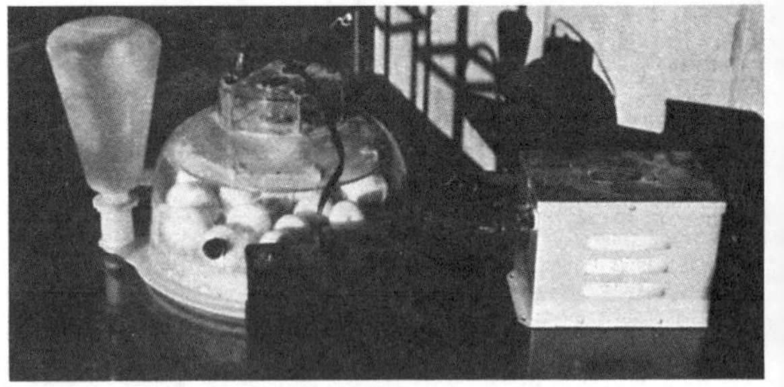

Small electrically heated, fan-forced incubator with automatic turning. Left to right: *water vessel, incubator, automatic turner, transformer.*

Setting tray tilted forward to show structure. Eggs placed point down in the egg compartment of the setting tray. Hatching tray lifted out to show structure.

Shows fan to move heated air around the incubator. The carbon filament heating lamps are seen to the left and right over the top of the incubator's water trays.

The broody hen

Many fanciers feel that the incubator is an unnecessary expense when a broody hen can be used, and prefer to use this natural method.

How an incubator works

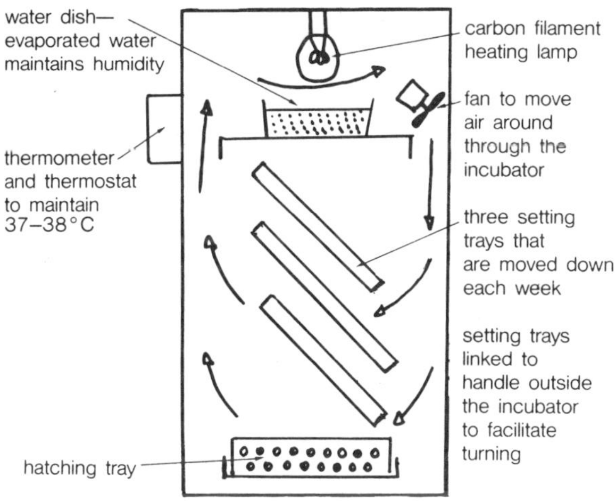

On the 18th day the eggs are candled (check their fertility) and placed in the hatching tray. The chickens should be left to hatch undisturbed.

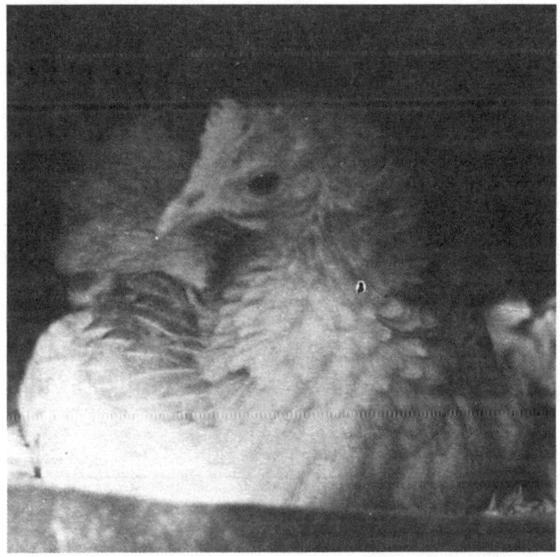

Broody bantam hen. Notice the ruffled feathers.

Setting a broody is not a difficult operation, and chickens can be hatched this way with little trouble provided a few guidelines are adhered to.

1. The broody hen should be shifted at night away from the remainder of the females to a quiet pen where she will experience little disturbance.
2. She should be left with a few eggs (not the eggs to be set) to ensure that she is truly broody and will sit. The true broody hen will ruffle her feathers, squark or cluck and peck out at any intruder including humans. Refer to the photo of the broody bantam hen.
3. When convinced she is firmly set, that evening carefully exchange the eggs she is sitting on for your fertile eggs.

Make sure she has access to fresh water and preferably feed her grain each day rather than layer pellets as the grain is less likely to scour her (runny droppings), resulting in a messy, smelly nest. Normally she will leave the nest of an evening if you feed her some grain, have a drink, do her droppings outside the nest and then return to sitting.

5. Dust the hen and the surrounding nest litter with an approved lice powder to prevent external parasite build up whilst she is sitting.
6. Avoid disturbing the hen at hatching time to prevent her from accidentally treading on the hatching chickens.

Natural versus artificial incubation

Poultry fanciers spend much time debating which method is best. Here we shall look at some of the points for and against each method. The final decision is a personal one based on what best suits your own situation, level of interest and the amount of money you are prepared to outlay.

Checking egg fertility

This is referred to by poultry fanciers as 'candling'. It involves shining a beam of light through the egg to see if there is a chicken developing inside it. Candling can be done by using a thin beam of

Point to be considered	*Broody hen*	*Incubator*
1. Capital outlay	Little	Large
2. Reliability	Variable—some are excellent, particularly Silkies, Silkie crosses or bantams, whilst others are most unreliable	Barring electrical failures, reliability good
3. Availability	Not always available when needed	More readily available
4. Labour input	None except at feeding time	Depending on the type of incubator, regular checking, turning and water topping up is required
5. Disease control	Difficult with external parasites and impossible with diseases such as Marek's Disease	Can be fumigated to kill disease organisms. Separates young from old, so the benefits of vaccination can be had
6. Chicken numbers achieved	Only small numbers hatched unless many broodies available	Depending on size of incubator, large numbers can be hatched at one time. This makes it easier to assemble like grower groups later

Candling eggs

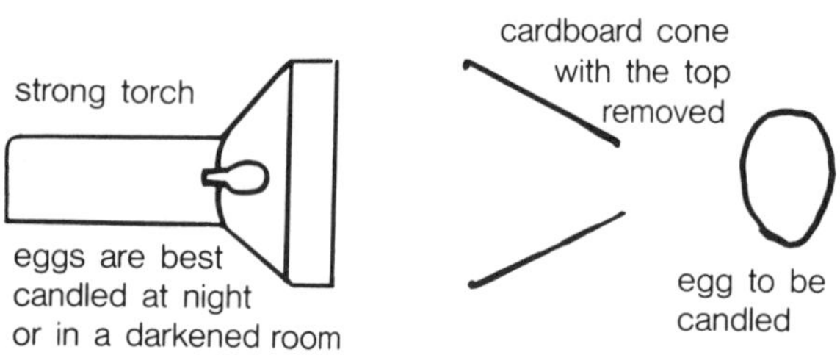

Appearance of eggs during candling

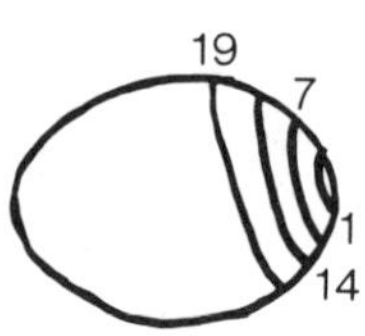

This diagram shows the increase in the egg's air space during incubation.

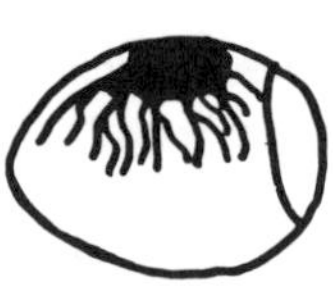

The development likely to be seen after 7 days of incubation.

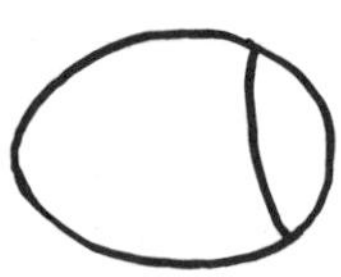

As incubation proceeds, the area containing the embryo darkens. By the 18th day the embryo is opaque.

sunlight shining between two curtains through a window into a darkened room. Another simple method is to use a torch and a cardboard cone with the pointed top removed to concentrate the light through the egg. See the accompanying diagram 'Candling Eggs'. It is important not to use a strong light or the accompanying heat could damage the developing embryo inside the egg. Using the torch method, a broody's eggs can be candled at night, and any that do not appear to be developing disposed of.

The poultry fancier should candle the eggs he has set at two main points of incubation:

1. The first is after 7 days and any eggs that fail to show development are usually disposed of.
2. On the 18th day when the eggs in the incubator are transferred from the setting trays to the hatching trays where they are left undisturbed while the chickens hatch.

The main changes in appearance are as follows (see diagram 'Appearance of eggs during candling'):

1. The air cell increases in size until it occupies some 25% of the internal volume of the egg by the 19th day in large fowls.
2. The rest of the interior of the egg appears much darker until it becomes a dark opaque mass by the 19th day.

3. Earlier in incubation, blood vessels may be seen around the yolk region.
4. The infertile egg has a distinctly clear appearance.

With a little practise, candling of eggs becomes a simple operation and one that fascinates children, particularly if they see the developing embryo moving around inside the egg.

Development of the embryo chicken

The following table gives a summary of the major developments inside the egg over the incubation period.

Day	*Major developments in the embryo*
1	Germ spot (zygote) enlarges forming a round clear area on the yolk. This is called the blastoderm.
2	A line called the primitive streak develops across the blastoderm. Blood vessels start to grow out from the streak across the yolk.
3	Heart has formed and is beating. Blood vessels grow further across the yolk to gather food for the developing chicken.
4	Brain has started to develop. Eye is also forming on the side of the head.
5	The tail of the embryo starts to form limb buds.
6	Heart moved into the chest cavity.
7	Neck appears. Beak starts to form.
8	Brain is enclosed in the skull. Beak has divided into upper and lower parts.
9	Toes start forming.
10	Lump on beak called 'pipping beak' or 'egg tooth' appears. This is needed later in hatching.
11	Embryo takes on a chick-like appearance.
12	Ear opening now formed. Feathers begin to appear.
13	Toe nails and leg scales appear on the legs.
14	Down feathers almost cover the body.
15	Head moves towards the hatching position under the right wing.
16	Egg white almost absorbed. The yolk is now the sole source of food.
17	Beak under the right wing points towards the egg's air cell.
18	Chicken is fully developed and prepared to hatch.
19	Beak breaks into the air cell and the chick starts to breathe air. Yolk remains absorbed through the navel.
20	Navel heals over. Shell 'pipped' as the chicken's beak breaks through. It now breathes air from outside the egg. The chicken rotates inside the shell, using its wing as a guide, and pushes out a circular break around the large end of the egg.
21	The chicken then pushes the top off and scrambles free of the shell. It dries and fluffs up.

Brooding

Brooding means caring for the newly hatched chickens through to when they have a covering of feathers at six to eight weeks of age. This involves taking them from dependence on the stable environment of the hatching tray to a stage where they can feed themselves and handle a range of temperatures. What are the basic needs that have to be met?

1. Warmth
2. Water
3. Food
4. Adequate ventilation but free of draughts
5. Dry litter on which to run
6. A restraint or hover to keep the chickens near the heat source.

Warmth

In the case of the broody, it is the hen's body that provides the warmth for the chickens. Where chickens are hatched in an incubator, an artificial heat source will have to be used. The most convenient source would be a heating lamp either carbon filament or infra red. These will also provide adequate light for the chickens to find their food and water. To regulate the temperature of the brooder area, the lamp can be raised or lowered, giving a corresponding raising or lowering of the brooder area temperature. Without using a thermometer, the fancier can see whether the chickens are too hot or too cold by observing their behaviour. If they crowd and huddle immediately under the lamp, often emitting a piercing, distressed cheep, they are too cold. Under such conditions the lamp will need to be lowered or an additional lamp used. On the other hand, if the chickens are crowded as far away from the lamp as possible, with their wings drooped and panting with their beaks open, the brooder area is too hot. The lamp will have to be raised or turned off for a period of time. If the chickens are at a comfortable temperature, they are evenly spread across the brooder area, either sleeping or actively scratching and searching for food.

At first the temperature will have to be as close as possible to that of the hatching tray in the incubator, 37–38°C. Always pre-heat the brooder area before taking chickens from the incubator. As the chickens age, the lamp can be raised to lower the brooder temperature and speed up feathering. In the later stages of brooding, it should be possible to turn the lamp off during the day and only give heat at night.

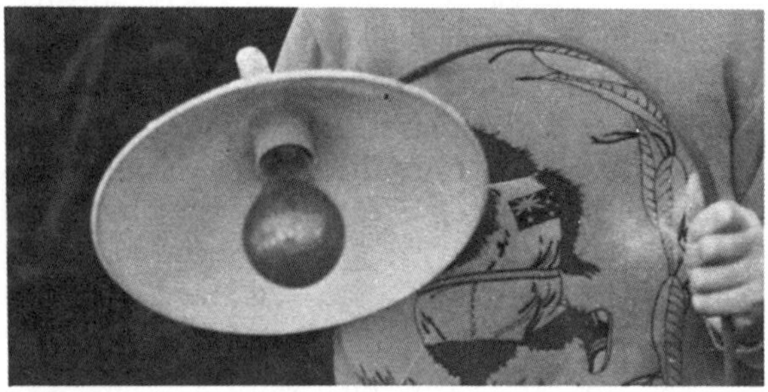

Shroud to direct heat down on to chickens in the brooder.

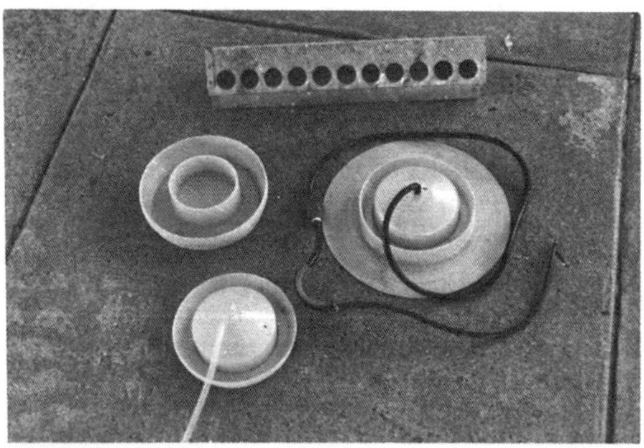

Chicken brooding equipment. Three examples of shallow round drinkers. Also included is a covered chicken feeder to prevent chickens scratching out their food.

It is a good idea to have a metal shroud over the top of the heating lamp to direct the heat down onto the chickens. It also serves to protect the heating lamp against accidental breakage.

Water

Since the chickens are brooded at relatively high temperatures, they will have a relatively high water need (thirst) and will not tolerate long periods without water, so a clean supply should be available at all times. The other problem with young chickens is that the water dish must not be too deep, otherwise they will fall in, become drenched and more easily chill. At worst they could drown. Chicks therefore, will need a shallow dish, preferably one they cannot get into. Such drinkers are shown in the photograph 'Chicken brooding equipment'.

Food

Young chickens can survive up to 48 hours after hatching on the yolk remains absorbed through the navel shortly before hatching. This explains why day old chickens can be transported long distances in the 24 hours after they leave the incubator. A point to remember is not to rush newly hatched chickens out of the incubator. Allow them time to fully strengthen up as they have the yolk remains to live on.

Special attention must be paid to food offered to chicks. For the sake of convenience it is best to use a commercially prepared chick starter crumble. These have been formulated to provide a high level of protein and energy as well as essential vitamins and minerals in a small particle size that is easy for the chicks to eat. Chick starter is more expensive than other food but since the amount the chicks eat is so small, the added expense is worth it. As well, chick starter contains a chemical (coccidiostat) to slow the effects of the coccidia organism; coccidiosis can be devastating to young chickens as they have little or no resistance to it.

Food must be given in containers to prevent the chicks either scratching litter into the food or getting into it themselves, soiling it or scratching it out of the containers. Such food containers are shown in the photograph 'Chicken brooding equipment'.

Adequate ventilation

The chicken brooder should preferably be located

in a shed or garage which prevents cold breezes chilling the chickens. However, the brooder should have sufficient air movement to prevent the air in it becoming stuffy and low in oxygen. Chicks kept in such conditions are more likely to become sick.

Dry litter

Chickens should be kept on a dry litter of shavings or rice hulls at all times. Should any part of the litter become damp, particularly around drinkers, it should be removed and replaced with dry litter. A good idea is to place the drinker on a piece of plastic large enough to cover the immediate litter area around it. Damp litter is an ideal site for the coccidia organism to become infective.

A restraint or hover

This is a barrier that keeps young chickens near the source of heat, food and water in the first two weeks or so until they become familiar with their surroundings. The barrier can be made of metal, fibro, chicken wire or bags. A useful material is a 50 cm strip of flat galvanised iron sheet metal which can be curved around into a circle to contain the young chicks around the heat lamp. After about two weeks the hover can be removed and the chicks will then move in and out of the heated area as they choose.

The principles of a simple brooder are shown in the diagram 'Simple Chicken Brooder'.

At this stage, we should mention the broody hen and her chickens. Around 24 hours after the eggs were due to hatch, and if there is no evidence of further hatching, the hen and chickens are best shifted into a small broody pen. This can be positioned on the lawn where it can be shifted onto a new area of grass each day. The hen and chicks will still need food and water supplied as outlined for raising chickens artifically. It will be necessary to place a bag over the pen to afford some protection against the wind and rain. See photograph showing a suitable broody pen for a bantam hen and chickens.

Small portable broody cage suitable for a bantam hen and chickens. It can be moved across the lawn to offer a fresh pick each day.

Once the chickens have reached bout 8 to 12 weeks of age and are well feathered, they can be

Simple chicken brooder

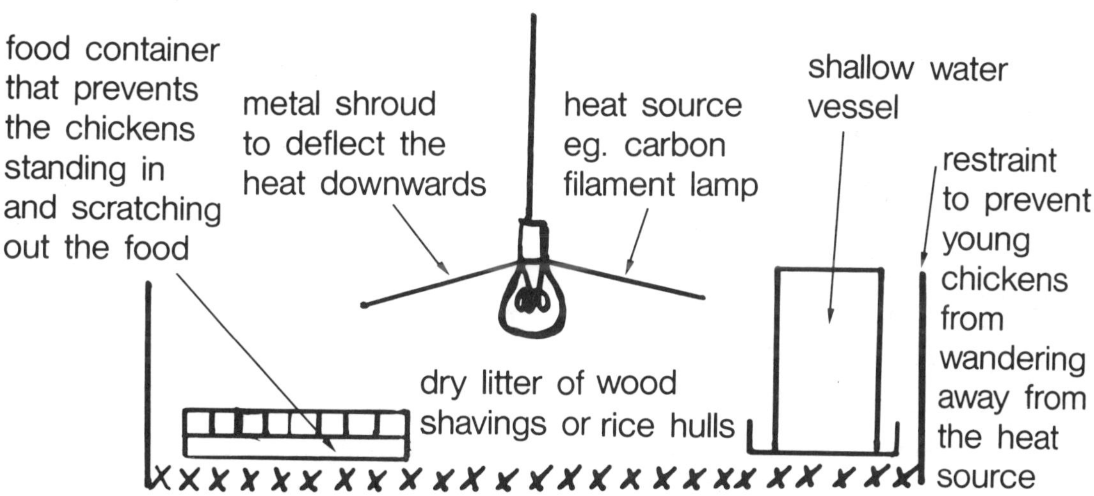

separated from the hen and treated as growers that have been artificially raised.

Raising chickens to adulthood

This phase of raising fowls starts with the 6 to 8 weeks old chicken from the brooder and ends with the fully grown cockerel or the pullet about to lay (point of lay). The fowls during this phase are called growers. Some important husbandry steps must be undertaken to ensure that the desired end result is achieved i.e. fit and healthy young adult stock. The following points need consideration:

1. feeding and watering
2. isolation from older stock
3. separation of the sexes
4. sufficient space
5. regular culling
6. a disease and pest control program.

Feeding

The protein needs of pure breed fowls is lower during this phase of growth with most grower rations being around 15% protein, whereas chick starter crumbles are around 20% protein. It is a fallacy to think that the fowls will grow faster using high protein and energy foods such as broiler rations. The fowl's genetic makeup determines how quickly it will grow and no matter how much extra protein is fed, it will not grow any faster; in fact, the protein will be wasted. If such high protein/energy rations are used, the net result is a fat flabby grower. The diet should be tailored to cater for the fowl's maximum nutritional needs and no more. On the other hand, growth and development will be slowed if there is a protein short-fall. Some astute and experienced fanciers manipulate grower rations to suit special end needs, but it is better for the beginner to feed a recognised commercial grower ration and avoid all danger of incorrect feeding.

As with all classes of fowls, growers should have continuous access to clean cool water. If the fowls are kept on a semi-intensive deep litter system, they can now use the adult automatic drinkers. Young fowls that are raised in moveable grower pens on a lawn will need drinkers and feeders into which they cannot get. A practical solution to this problem is

Grower feeders with top to prevent growers getting into the feed tray.

An alternative grower drinker made from used ice-cream containers with lids. Holes large enough for a grower's head are cut into the sides.

to use plastic ice cream containers with elongated holes cut in the sides. The lids keep the birds out of the food and water.

Isolation from older stock

As mentioned in the earlier chapter on disease and pests of poultry, it is important to keep young and old stock separated as often older stock are carriers of disease that can be passed on to susceptible young stock when they are run together. Three important parasites readily transferred this way are worms, scaly leg mite and coccidia. As pointed out in the chapter on housing, it is preferable to raise young stock on ground or in yards that have been depopulated for at least four months. This effectively breaks the life cycle of most disease causing parasites.

When younger fowls are run with older stock, they tend to be picked on and bullied, thus occupying a low place in the social order of the yard. This means that they are chased away from the food and water containers, only being allowed there when no older fowls are around. Young fowls will not grow well under such conditions.

Separation of the sexes

As soon as possible after the 6 to 8 weeks stage, the young fowls should be separated into groups of the same sex and age with the desirable group size being around 12. This size is ideal for avoiding the development of a large social peck order. Even the lowest member of a group this size has a reasonable chance of doing well.

As the cockerels (young males) grow older, they may start fighting with permanent damage to the comb, wattles and lobes being done. Some fanciers use an older cock bird to act as a policeman to keep the peace and minimise fighting. Before such a bird is put in with young stock, he must be wormed, deloused and treated with sulfaquinoxaline to make sure he is free of any transmissible pests and diseases.

If a particular fowl, male or female looks like being an outstanding prospect, many fanciers remove it from the grower group and place it in a separate small pen or yard where it can grow and develop without the risk of injury or damage caused by its peers. This is particularly important with breeds which have showy head gear and long flowing tails for example Leghorns, Hamburghs and Rosecombs.

Sufficient space

As pointed out in the chapter on housing, one of the main problems for beginners is that they do not allow enough space to run their growing stock. This can mean that the carefully bred and hatched stock do not have the space to fully develop and reach their potential. This generally shows as poorly feathered growers. With sufficient space between the birds rapid feathering occurs and feather picking is minimised. There is nothing more frustrating than to have growers picking the feather buds out of the tails and backs of other birds.

Young birds need the space to exercise their young developing bodies. This can be aided by a good deep dry litter in which to scratch. Scratching can be encouraged by introducing growers to a small amount of grain, but not too much as the grain is of lower protein than the grower ration. If the young fowls fill themselves with grain, their growth rate is slowed.

Many game fowl breeders also like to provide high roosts to encourage their fowls to fly and exercise their wings. The scratching and flying condition the birds and this is reflected in their handling, a point of major importance when judging game fowls.

Fanciers of heavy breeds avoid giving growers roosts as they produce a breast dent in the breast bone. This is caused by the roost deforming the young cartilaginous breast bone which, at that particular stage, has not hardened. If you look at the typical broiler (meat) chicken sold in the supermarket, when cooked, you notice that the breastbone is soft and rubbery. It is during this stage of the bird's growth that the damage is done. Once the bone hardens as the bird ages, the dent becomes permanent. This can go against the bird later in the show pen. Heavy breed fanciers therefore free range their growers or raise them on a deep litter system.

Regular culling

This means removing any fowl with an obvious fault that is not likely to go away as the bird ages. Obvious physical faults include wrong colour, deformities and runts. Culling is an on going process that really starts at day old but is very important in the grower stage where birds that have little future prospect can be weeded out before they eat too much food or occupy unnecessary space. Some culls are killed if they have major faults, whilst others may be sold off if the faults are minor to offset the food bill. Obviously a high price cannot be asked for these. It is worthwhile remembering that poultry raising is one of the few hobbies where you can eat your mistakes!

Disease control program

Disease control measures outlined in the chapter on pests and diseases must be adhered to, as young fowls are most susceptible, and their growth may be adversely affected if they become ill. Most older fowls have built up resistance to disease, but this takes time. It is therefore important to carry out the vaccinations on time, and regularly dust for external parasites and worm for internal ones.

This phase of poultry raising lays the foundations for next season's breeding stock and show team, so it requires a deal of thought and planning by the fancier. It is the biggest hurdle for both the young and those new to the fancy to overcome. If this challenge is met, it can be one of the most satisfying aspects of poultry raising.

An alternative way of using the Multiplo system

The multiplo incubator can be used as a 'setting cabinet' for the first eighteen days and on the nineteenth day, the incubator be used as a 'hatching cabinet'. This means that all setting trays are set at the same time rather than on a weekly basis as previously outlined. Also it necessitates buying extra hatching trays to slide into the setting spaces. To use the setting spaces, the standard hatching trays have to be modified slightly to fit into the space in the setting section. The standard hatching tray will stack two trays high in the bottom of the incubator with the setting rack in the horizontal position. This in itself doubles the hatching space available in the bottom of the incubator. For those with a little ingenuity, substitute hatching trays can be made from one centimetre by one centimetre metal fabric weave to slide into the setting space. When using hatching trays on top of each other, ensure paper towelling is used on the bottom of each tray to prevent droppings and other material dropping down into the tray below.

There are some useful practical advantages of using the incubator this way. Firstly, it eliminates the change in humidity during the hatching phase and subjecting the trays of eggs in the setting phase to a period of higher humidity than that required during the setting phase. Excessive humidity during the setting phase is known to affect the developing chick adversely. Secondly, all chickens are the same age making it easier to set up groups of growers of similar size thus reducing feather picking and the adverse affects of peck order development amongst growers. Thirdly, it allows a large enough batch of chickens to be hatched to take economical advantage of the various vaccine packs.

The biggest disadvantage is not always having fresh setting eggs available when fitting the incubator. It also means a three week break between the setting of eggs. The fertility rate of the older eggs can possibly be diminished.

9 Preparing of Fowls for Exhibition

Show preparation is aimed at improving the appearance and behaviour of your birds prior to penning on show day when they should be seen at their best. It should show the results of many months of your endeavours and is regarded by many as the final step in the year's breeding program.

For many astute breeders, show preparation starts back at the breeding pen where they carefully calculate to have birds of a specific age available for a certain show. Some leading breeders believe that a female is at her best around the point of lay and at her peak for a period of 6 to 8 weeks. The breeder carefully calculates back from a future show date to know when he has to have a breeding pen together and eggs set for incubation so as to have fowls at their peak on that show date.

As mentioned in the previous chapter on raising growers, the breeder must keep an eye out for any potential show birds and separate these from the other growers to prevent any permanent damage to head gear or feathers. Damage at this stage to combs, wattles and lobes will be permanent and the only future for such birds is in the breeding pen. Many potential show champions have been permanently ruined at this stage. Feather damage is of a less permanent nature but will mean that the bird will miss the first show season and will have to wait until it has moulted to replace the damaged feathers. With some breeds, where the fowl is at its best as a pullet or cockerel, it may well ruin its show career as well.

Assuming we have a number of potential youngsters sorted out for exhibition, we now turn our attention to the pre-show preparation that is aimed at improving the bird's appearance and show pen behaviour.

Improved appearance versus faking

At this stage a clear distinction must be made between 'faking', which is liable to lead to the disqualification of the exhibit, and 'improved appearance' which means enhancing the bird's natural qualities. Common forms of faking that have been attempted by less reputable people include the following practices:

1. Colouring white ear lobes with red texta pen where red lobes are needed.
2. Using food colouring to gain a desired leg colour.
3. Replacing roosters sickle feathers. This involves the placing of a match stick up the shaft of the feather and replacing it in the butt of the removed sickle feather.
4. Oiling the feathers of certain game fowls.

Fortunately, poultry judges are experienced poultry-men, on the lookout for such undesirable practices, and will not hesitate to disqualify such birds where clear evidence of faking is found. More importantly, faking does not do the fancier's reputation any good, and once the word spreads about a case of faking, such cases are not forgotten for a long time. Faking is no substitute for good breeding, feeding and poultry management.

Pre-show poultry management

Potential show fowls must be well fed. This is reflected in the bird's condition and 'bloom'. Correct feeding of birds with glossy feathers such as Old English Game will ensure that there is plenty of shine in their feathers. A weekly supplement of an oil seed such as sunflower will bring out the feather shine.

Some fanciers advocate the feeding of corn to coloured birds to enrich their feather colour and in some cases, their leg colour. Whilst some may argue that this is in a sense faking, it is more a case of skilful feeding using a part of the bird's natural diet. Artificial colouring agents deliberately added to foods does constitute faking, and whilst this is harder to detect, tell tale signs of such activities are present in such birds if they are looked at closely.

If a fancier bases the bulk of the bird's diet on a commercially prepared ration, either grower for the young growing fowls or high quality layer crumbles for adults supplemented with fresh green feed and some grain, most breeds will not be nutritionally deficient.

Potential exhibition fowls should be regularly wormed either with individual worming capsules or with medicated drinking water. Worms quickly check a young bird's growth and condition. If left unwormed, the bird will soon lose its healthy bloom and appearance.

Show prospects should be housed in quarters that have been sprayed with an approved insecticidal solution such as Malathion® to eliminate any external parasites. The fowls should be regularly dusted with louse powder as an added precaution.

Many breeds benefit from being housed in shaded conditions out of direct sunlight to prevent fading of feather colour. Strong sunlight may bleach the colour or in some cases, change the feather colour. It also dries the natural shine oils out of the feather giving the fowl a dry bleached-out appearance called 'loss of bloom'.

Leg feathered breeds and some low statured soft feather bantam breeds not only need shaded conditions but also a deep dry litter of absorbent material such as wood shavings. This type of litter is beneficial to all breeds, but is particularly important to the above mentioned types to prevent spoilage of their leg feathers, especially around their feet, as well as the belly feathers.

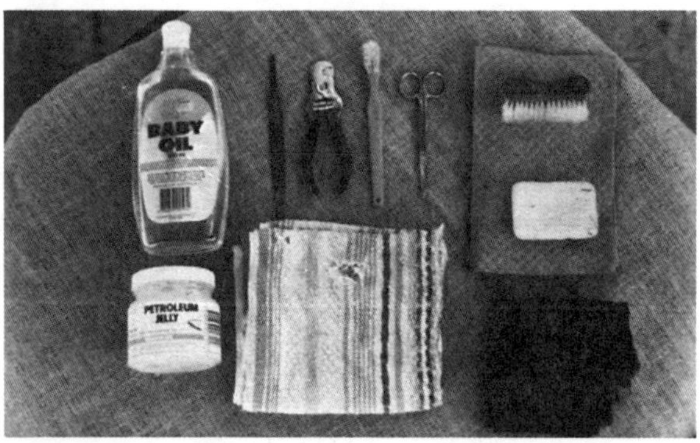

Show preparation equipment. Top left to right: *baby oil, fine file, nail cutters, toothbrush, fine pointed scissors, sponge, nail brush and pure soap.* Bottom: *petroleum jelly, towelling and silk cloth.*

Care of legs

A well prepared, clean pair of legs sets off any breed. Those leg feathered breeds will also need attention to their leg feathers, with regular washing to ensure the feathers do not become stained and vary greatly in colour from the rest of the bird's feather colour pattern.

The scale covered shanks and toes require careful attention. This job is best started well before the show, two or three weeks with young fowls but may go back to moulting time with older stock. The aim of the exercise is to have clean tight fitting scales on the shanks and toes. It is a job that takes time and cannot be rushed. When done properly it sets the bird off.

With older birds, check them at moulting time to see that the old scales are coming away. A wash and a scrub with a soft nail brush using warm soapy water at this time can be of great benefit. Remember the new scales underneath will be tender so when cleaning is finished, smear the shanks and toes with petroleum jelly. This prevents the scales hardening too much later and making subsequent cleaning more difficult. A monthly smearing of a mixture of petroleum jelly and yellow sulfur powder conditions the legs and stops scaly leg mite burrowing under the scale.

Both young and old birds can now be given similar pre-show leg treatment. Two or three weeks prior to a show, the bird's legs need to be soaked in warm water to soften them. If the bird is wrapped in a large old towel, it will prevent wetting the rest of the bird. The following steps can now be undertaken:

1. With a nail brush or an old tooth brush in the case of bantams, scrub the shanks and toes with plenty of soap.
2. If the nails are too long, trim them. A close examination of the nail will indicate how far back it is safe to cut without causing it to bleed. The sensitive part of the nail is a slightly different colour to the outer dead part. A cut just in front of this will not cause any bleeding.
3. The next step is to remove the dirt from under each scale. There is no substitute for time and patience here. To assist with this step, the tips of a fine pair of scissors, a nail or toothpick can be used to lift the scale gently and scrap out the dirt. The action is similar to cleaning your finger or toe

nails. With a little practice, the fancier becomes very adept at this job.

4. After the dirt has been removed from under the scales, a follow up scrubbing with soap and water will usually give the desired results. However any persistent dirt may have to be removed by a second scraping under the scales.

5. When the scales are clean, a liberal application of baby oil will penetrate to the bases of the scales and soothe any irritated tissue. On top of this apply a generous application of petroleum jelly. Wipe off any excess so it does not spoil the feathers.

Pen training

This is a necessity if a bird is to stand and display its qualities to advantage. Many a top quality bird has been overlooked at judging time because of a failure in this regard. Training must start well before the show season. Regular visits to the grower pens of an evening and a small amount of grain starts building confidence that humans will not harm them.

To successfully pen train the fowls, pens similar to show pens and preferably ones with show fronts should be used. Some successful exhibitors have a separate pen room with a light where the birds can be trained at night. Under subdued light they are more responsive to handling and train much more quickly. For the beginner who does not have such pen room facilities, the birds should be shifted to their training facilities at night, with a bag being placed over the front of the cage and left there for the first few days of training.

At first, every time you visit the bird give it some grain to build up its trust in you. Once it is reasonably settled, put your hand in the pen and catch and handle the bird several times so that it sees that no harm will come to it. Remember, after each session give it some grain. With the bird reasonably calm it is now time to start stick training it. A piece of thin dowel stick 50 cm long makes a good training stick.

It will not be long before the bird realises that the stick represents no threat, provided you place it in the cage when giving it some grain. Avoid poking at the bird, making sudden movements with the stick or hitting the bird with it. Run the stick gently across its back and across its front at first. After this has been mastered, it is possible to stroke the throat in order to encourage the bird to lift its head and display its type. Finally, it should be possible to move the bird around to where you want it with the stick. Some birds train better than others, but there is no substitute for time, patience and a reward of grain.

A technique often used with game fowls to catch them in a pen. The hand locks the wing and thigh together over the back. The fowl is then drawn head first towards you. The fowl is always brought head first towards the door of the pen. When returning the bird to the pen, it is always placed in the pen head first: this prevents damage to the bird's feathers.

Capturing soft feather fowls. Wing and thigh on the left side of the fowl are grasped together. The fowl is brought forward towards the pen door, leaving the left hand free to assist with bringing the bird out head first. As with game fowls, soft feather fowls are returned to pens head first.

The fowl is carried on the hand, wrist and forearm. The fingers have the legs firmly locked together. The other arm is free to assist with controlling the bird.

Shows the fowl in the carrying position.

Showing the bird held in position for examination of head features.

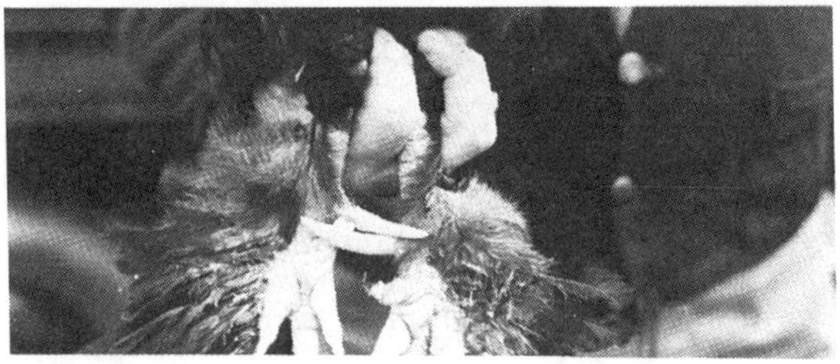

Closeup showing fingers and thumb firmly locking the fowl's legs together whilst the fowl is in the carrying position.

Bird held in position to examine its wings and wing feathering.

Washing

To the uninitiated this may seem ridiculous, but when one realises that *all* animal exhibits displayed at major shows are washed, it seems less so. Some colours of fowls need more washing than others, especially the white and light shades. Soft feather fowls need more washing than hard feather fowls, particularly breeds such as Silkies and Pekins.

This job is best done two to three days before the show to allow the birds time to preen the feathers into their natural position. Washing can be divided into three main steps: soaping, rinsing and drying. It is best to choose a sunny day when washing as it lessens the chance of the birds chilling. However, birds can be prepared at night provided some form of heating is used to assist drying.

Three tubs are needed for this job. Make sure they are large enough to comfortably take the fowl. Many good fowls have been ruined by being forced into a small washing tub. Tub one is the soaping tub; tub two is the first rinse tub; tub three is the final rinse tub, and for the preparation of white fowls, will have an amount of laundry blue placed in it to brighten the white feathers. The water for all tubs should be warm, around the fowl's body temperature, so test it before attempting to wash one.

Soaping

Use a mild pure soap or a good quality hair shampoo. Do not use harsh laundry detergents as the results are too severe on the feathers and tend to cause excessive irritation to the fowl.

Wash the feet with a brush or cloth before plunging the fowl in the soaping tub, and immersing it so as to saturate the feathers. Keep the head above water. A sponge cloth can be used to wash the comb, face, wattles and lobes. Lather up the neck, back through to the tail, wings, vent, breast and underneath in that order. The fowl will have to be removed from the tub while it is being lathered up, then returned to the soaping tub. A gentle scrubbing in the direction of the feathers may be necessary for stubbornly dirty patches. A re-lather of those patches may also be needed.

Rinsing

Lift the fowl from the soaping tub and drain. Plunge it in the first rinsing tub to remove all visible traces of soap and the shampoo. Lift and drain. Plunge the fowl in the second rinse tub. Lift and drain the bird.

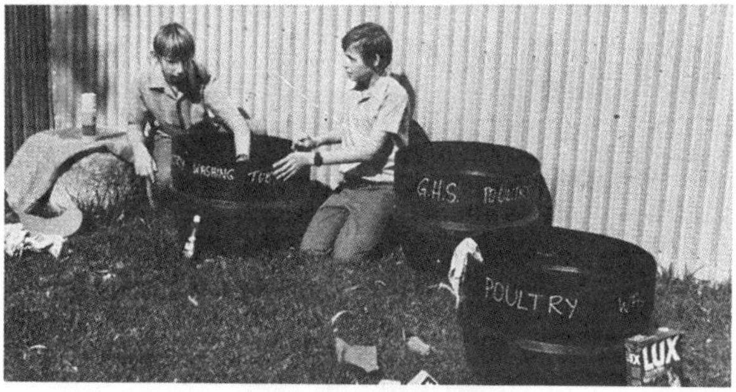

Show preparation. The three tubs needed to wash fowls. From the right: *soaping tub, first rinse tub and final rinse tub. The bag over the cement block is where the bird stands for sponging off excess water from the final rinse.*

Stage one of washing: fowl being soaped in the soaping tub.

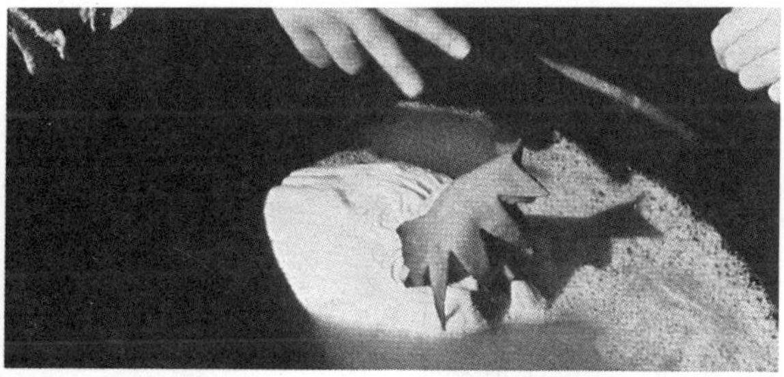

Close-up of White Leghorn in soaping tub.

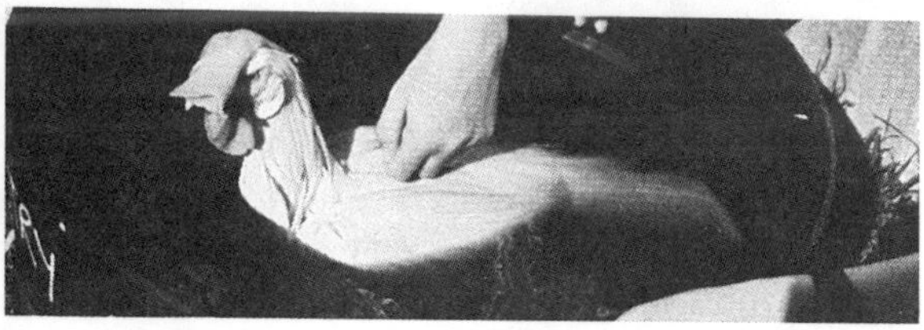

Close-up of White Leghorn in final rinse tub.

Drying

The bird should have excess water removed with towelling or sponges. An electric hair dryer can now be used to hasten the drying process. Starting along the back, direct the hot air to the base of the feathers, running your fingers through the feathers as you would your own hair when using a hair dryer. Avoid trying to fully dry the feathers in one spot but rather move evenly over the bird using your fingers to allow hot air to the feather bases. Do not attempt to achieve complete dryness or you will end up with a 'frizzed' fowl with feathers that refuse to sit properly. It is best to reach about a 80–90% dryness and then allow the bird to dry naturally in the sun or in a warmed room. The dried bird should be penned on dry coarse litter such as straw or wood shavings.

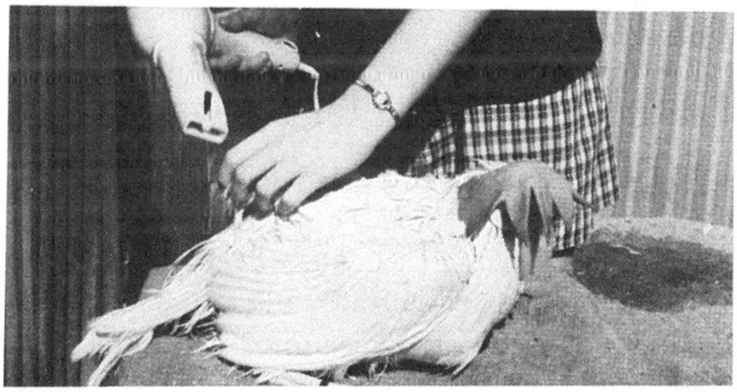

Blow drying following sponging down of excess water. Note student using her fingers to make sure warm air reaches the base of the feathers first.

Allowing the White Leghorn female to dry in the sun after reaching 80–90% dryness. Note tethering.

Group of White Leghorns tethered and drying in the sun on the lawn.

Final preparation

This involves attention to the head and legs the night before the show.

Head The comb, wattles, lobes and face are gently washed with a warm sponge then carefully dried. These are then brightened up with an application of petroleum jelly or oil such as olive or baby oil. Any excess should be carefully wiped away.

Legs The legs are wiped clean with a warm moist sponge or rag, then dried. An application of petroleum jelly or oil is given with the excess being removed.

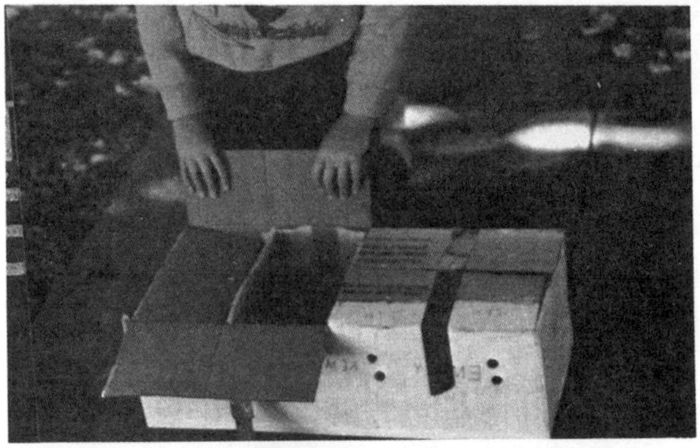

Cardboard boxes suitable for taking bantams to shows. Boxes lined with a deep litter of shavings.

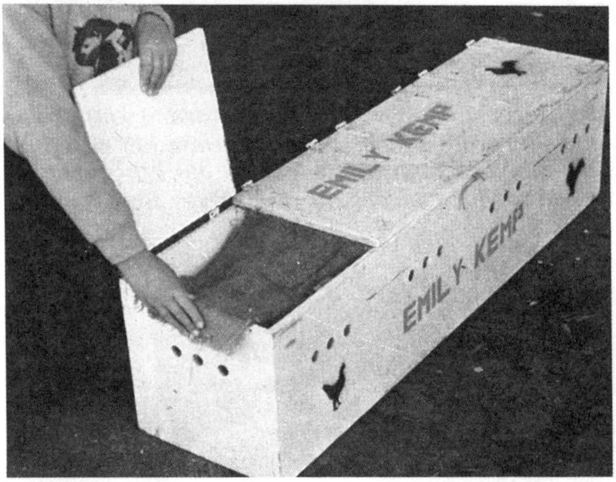

Custom made boxes to fit across a box trailer.

Transport to the show

Each bird is best transported in its own box or compartment of a box. The bottom of the box should be covered in clean absorbent litter to soak up droppings passed during transport. The box or compartment size should comfortably house the bird without cramping it.

Boxes can range from good quality cardboard boxes to elaborate custom made models. Either extreme does the same job. For the beginner, sturdy cardboard boxes are sufficient, for they are cheap and easily obtainable. Some fanciers have special boxes made to fit the boot of their car or trailer. They are a luxury the beginner can decide on at a later date.

Where large numbers of fowls need to be transported, a trailer may have to be used. Here fanciers often make boxes to exactly fit the trailer to make loading and stacking easier. The trailer needs to be well tarped, and the more committed to the fancy have custom made tarpaulins made to avoid trailer covers coming adrift in their rush to a show. It is also advisable to lower the pressure in the trailer tyres, to give some cushioning over bumps. There are no shock absorbers on a standard box trailer and this can mean a jolty ride for the birds.

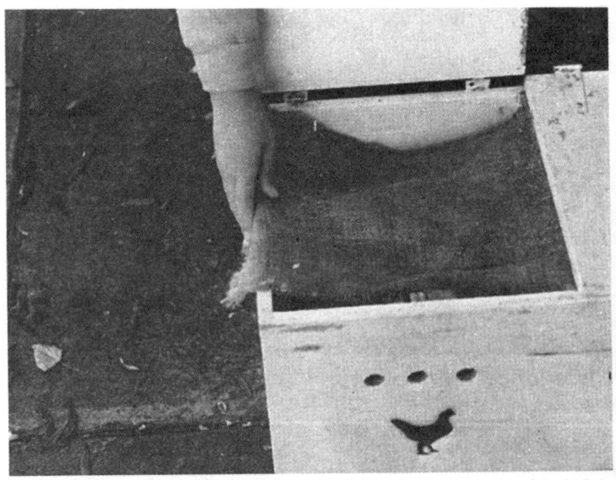

Hessian cover to prevent fowl flying out when the lid is opened.

A point to bear in mind, whether the fowls are transported in the boot, or in a covered trailer, is not to leave birds for long periods of time in a closed car boot or covered trailer exposed to full sunlight. They heat up very quickly to high temperatures and people have been known to lose birds through their own carelessness in this regard.

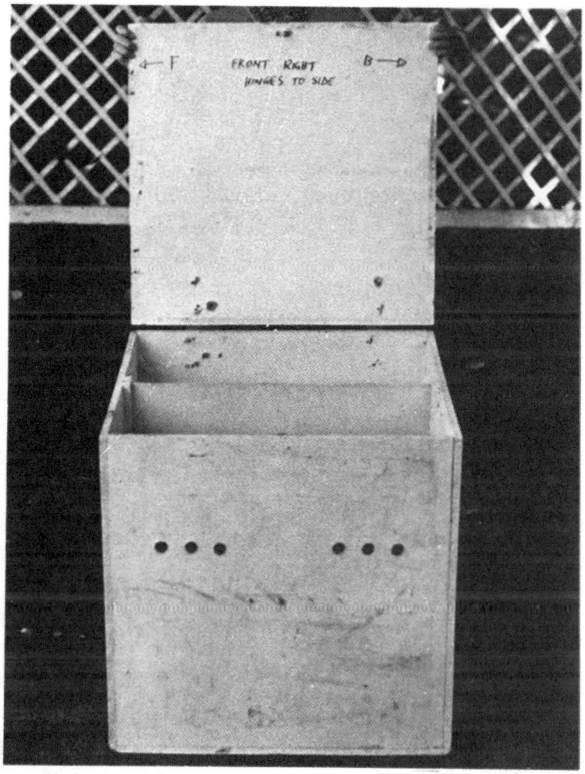

Large fowl carrying box suitable for transporting two large roosters.

Interior of large fowl carrying box. Note it has removable division to make the box suitable for transporting large tailed fowls such as Leghorn roosters.

Trailer set up for carrying large numbers of fowls to poultry shows. The picture shows a wide variety of carrying boxes.

Samples of poultry exhibitors' transport outside the Wagga Poultry Pavilion.

On arrival at the poultry pavilion

Barring accidents in transit, this should be a simple check on the birds' condition just prior to placing them in their allocated show pens.

1. Check their legs and remove any droppings they have trodden in during transport. A final wipe with an oily rag (olive or baby) is beneficial.
2. The comb wattles and lobes may need a final touch with oil but remove any excess.
3. Check for soiled vents. Some fowls travel better than others. Fowls with a soiled vent will need a 'patch up' job, so it is a good idea to carry a dish-washer brush for removing most of the soiling material from the feathers. A roll of disposable paper towel is excellent for the remaining mopping up. Scouring (runny droppings) can be reduced if the grain intake is increased and green feed stopped two days before the show.
4. Some fowls benefit from a final wipe down over the wings and body with a silk cloth or soft towelling just prior to placing in the show pen.

To conclude this chapter on the preparation of fowls for exhibition the following points should be remembered:

1. Preparation starts a long time before the show.
2. Good poultry husbandry is needed to produce potential show fowls.
3. The actual preparation is time consuming.
4. Much patience is required to prepare show fowls.
5. It is better to take a small team of well prepared fowls than a large number of poorly prepared fowls as they reflect on you.

10 Showing Poultry

Poultry shows

There are two main types: the poultry club shows and the agricultural society shows. The differences are as follows:

Poultry club shows are run by a poultry club over the May–June–July–August period. They are held in a showground pavilion and feature poultry only. In some cases, duck, goose, turkey and guinea fowl sections are provided. Trophies and/or prize money is raised from the entry fees which must accompany the entry forms. This type of show has none of the other attractions associated with agricultural shows; it is a specialist show.

On the other hand, agricultural shows are generally held in autumn or spring with the poultry section being only part of a range of classes provided for sheep, cattle, horses and farm produce, etc. The agricultural society raises the prize money and their entry fees are much lower than for a poultry club show. Major awards at these shows are keenly sought after by poultry fanciers, particularly as many agricultural societies still give out tri-coloured felt ribbons for major awards. These are trophies in themselves that most poultry clubs can no longer afford.

How do you know the shows are on?
There are a number of ways. Firstly, word of mouth when attending a show. Secondly, members from other clubs will often hand out schedules and entry forms for future shows. Thirdly, they are advertised in such publications as *The Fanciers' Gazette* published by the Bantam Club of NSW or *The Weekly Times* newspaper in the forthcoming show section. Fourthly, by contacting a poultry club secretary, who will also give you the address and telephone number of other club secretaries you wish to contact. Fifthly, once you have exhibited at a particular show, the secretary will send you a schedule the following year.

It does not take long for the word to get around that you are an exhibitor and you will find that after a short period of exhibiting fowls, you will receive more schedules to shows than you will be able to attend.

How to enter
Entries must be in the hands of the club or society secretary by the due date on the schedule. Remember, late entries are not appreciated, as much work has to be done before the fowls are penned on show morning. Most entry forms are in duplicate. The exhibitor must fill in both the secretary's copy on the left hand side and the exhibitor's copy on the right hand side. Both completed copies must be sent to the show secretary.

To complete the form, look up the class number for your breed and exhibit. Write this on your entry form as well as the particulars of the exhibit i.e. breed and sex and whether a cock or hen, or cockerel or pullet: the pen number column is left blank for the show secretary or chief steward to complete. The completed form along with the entry fees are then sent off to the show secretary. See the examples of part of a show schedule and an entry form.

Arrival on show day
Check the time judging starts on the schedule and plan to arrive at the pavilion sufficiently before this to allow for last minute preparations and penning of birds. On arrival at the pavilion, pick up the pen numbers from the show secretary. The pen numbers will be written on the exhibitor's copy of the entry form you sent to the secretary when entering your birds for the show.

Each pen in the pavilion will have a pen card with two numbers attached to it. The first is the class number found in the schedule and the second is the exhibit number. You look for your class number first, then check for your pen number on your entry form. You will now have the pen in which your exhibit is to be placed. It is a good idea to tick the birds off on your entry form as you pen them.

Schedule

1. Orpington Buff Cock
2. Orpington Buff Hen
3. Orpington Buff Cockerel
4. Orpington Buff Pullet
5. Orpington A.O.C. Cock
6. Orpington A.O.C. Hen
7. Orpington A.O.C.Cockerel
8. Orpington A.O.C. Pullet
9. White Wyandotte Cock
10. White Wyandotte Hen
11. White Wyandotte Cockerel
12. White Wyandotte Pullet
13. A.O.C. Wyandotte Cock
14. A.O.C. Wyandotte Hen
15. A.O.C. Wyandotte Cockerel
16. A.O.C. Wyandotte Pullet
17. Sussex A.C. Cock
18. Sussex A.C. Hen
19. Sussex A.C. Cockerel
20. Sussex A.C. Pullet
21. Australorp Cock
22. Australorp Hen
23. Australorp Cockerel
24. Australorp Pullet
25. Rhode Island Red Cock
26. Rhode Island Red Hen
27. Rhode Island Red Cockerel
28. Rhode Island Red Pullet
29. Rhode Island White Cock
30. Rhode Island White Hen
31. Rhode Island White Cockerel
32. Rhode Island White Pullet
33. Plymouth Rock Cock
34. Plymouth Rock Hen
35. Plymouth Rock Cockerel
36. Plymouth Rock Pullet
37. Langshan Chinese Black Cock
38. Langshan Chinese Black Hen
39. Langshan Chinese Black Cockerel
40. Langshan Chinese Black Pullet
41. Leghorn White Cock
42. Leghorn White Hen
43. Leghorn White Cockerel
44. Leghorn White Pullet
45. Leghorn Brown Cock
46. Leghorn Brown Hen
47. Leghorn Brown Cockerel
48. Leghorn Brown Pullet
49. Minorca Cock
50. Minorca Hen
51. Minorca Cockerel
52. Minorca Pullet
53. Ancona Cock
54. Ancona Hen
55. Ancona Cockerel
56. Ancona Pullet
57. Silkie A.C. Cock
58. Silkie A.C. Hen
59. Silkie A.C. Cockerel
60. Silkie A.C. Pullet
61. Hamburg Male
62. Hamburg Female
63. A.O.V. Not Mentioned Cock
64. A.O.V. Not Mentioned Hen
65. A.O.V. Not Mentioned Cockerel
66. A.O.V. Not Mentioned Pullet

Old English game classes

67. Black Red Light Legged Cock
68. Partridge Light Legged Hen
69. Black Red Light Legged Cockerel
70. Partridge Light Legged Pullet
71. Black Red Dark Legged Cock
72. Partridge Dark Legged Hen
73. Blach Red Dark Legged Cockerel
74. Partridge Dark Legged Pullet
75. Duckwing Light Legged Cock
76. Duckwing Light Legged Hen
77. Duckwing Light Legged Cockerel
78. Duckwing Light Legged Pullet
79. Duckwing Dark Legged Cock
80. Duckwing Dark Legged Hen
81. Duckwing Dark Legged Cockerel
82. Duckwing Dark Legged Pullet
83. Brown Red Cock
84. Brown Red Hen
85. Brown Red Cockerel
86. Brown Red Pullet
87. Grey or Birchen Cock
88. Grey or Birchen Hen
89. Grey or Birchen Cockerel
90. Grey or Birchen Pullet
91. Blue Red Light Legged Cock
92. Blue Red Light Legged Hen
93. Blue Red Light Legged Cockerel
94. Blue Red Light Legged Pullet
95. Blue Red Dark Legged Cock
96. Blue Red Dark Legged Hen
97. Blue Red Dark Legged Cockerel
98. Blue Red Dark Legged Pullet
99. Pile Cock
100. Pile Hen
101. Pile Cockerel
102. Pile Pullet
103. Black or Brassy Back Cock
104. Black or Brassy Back Hen
105. Black or Brassy Back Cockerel
106. Black or Brassy Back Pullet
107. O.E.G. A.O.C. Cock
108. O.E.G. A.O.C. Hen
109. O.E.G. A.O.C. Cockerel
110. O.E.G. A.O.C. Pullet
111. Indian Game Cock
112. Indian Game Hen
113. Indian Game Cockerel
114. Indian Game Pullet
115. Jubilee Cock
116. Jubilee Hen
117. Jubilee Cockerel
118. Jubilee Pullet
119. Australian Game Duckwing Cock
120. Australian Game Duckwing Hen
121. Australian Game Duckwing Cockerel
122. Australian Game Duckwing Pullet
123. Australian Game A.O.C. Cock
124. Australian Game A.O.C. Hen
125. Australian Game A.O.C. Cockerel
126. Australian Game A.O.C. Pullet
127. Pitt Game Male
128. Pitt Game Female

Breeding pairs

129. A.V. Soft Feather Heavy Pair
130. A.V. Soft Feather Light Pair
131. A.V. Game Pair
132. A.V. Hardfeather Pair (Bantam)
133. A.V. Softfeather Pair (Bantam)

BANTAM CLASSES SEE PAGE 2

If you have any doubts about your pens, check with the show secretary who will generally hand you over to the steward for the appropriate section to sort out any problems.

Should you be late arriving at a show, try to get a message to the show secretary if possible. Mostly, judging will be delayed in genuine cases, but not if no advice of your lateness has been given by judging time. Unnecessary delays irritate fellow exhibitors and judges alike.

Some shows allow penning of birds between specific hours on the evening prior to a show. This is generally indicated on the schedule, but it is advisable to notify the show secretary should you wish to pen early. The pavilion is then locked over night and reopened early next morning for early arrivers.

Judging

Today a system of open judging exists. This means that the exhibitors can watch a judge at work assessing the exhibits provided they do not make unnecessary noise or derogatory remarks while the judge is in action. This was not always the case. A system of 'closed judging' was practised, only the judge and his stewards (official helpers) being allowed in the pavilion at judging time; exhibitors had to remain outside. Many exhibitors felt the

SECRETARY'S COPY

ENTRY FORM

Class	Particulars of Exhibits	Pen No.
18	SUSSEX A.C. HEN	3
19	SUSSEX A.C. CKL	4
20	SUSSEX A.C. PLT	1
20	SUSSEX A.C. PLT	2
43	LEGHORN WHITE CKL	5
44	LEGHORN WHITE PLT	7

.... Entries @ .... -

Membership ...... -

Donation ...... -

TOTAL $ -

I hereby enter the above, subject to the Rules and Regulations of the Society.

Exhibitor's Full Initials, Name and Address in BLOCK LETTERS.

NAME GRIFFITH HIGH SCHOOL

ADDRESS P.O. BOX 1021
GRIFFITH 2680 N.S.W.

CLASS

44

PEN No

7

PEN CARD

EXHIBITOR'S COPY

ENTRY FORM

Class	Particulars of Exhibits	Pen No.
18	SUSSEX A.C. HEN	3
19	SUSSEX A.C. CKL	4
20	SUSSEX A.C. PLT	1
20	SUSSEX A.C. PLT	2
43	LEGHORN WHITE CKL	5
44	LEGHORN WHITE PLT	7

.... Entries @ .... -

Membership ...... -

Donation ...... -

TOTAL $ -

I hereby enter the above, subject to the Rules and Regulations of the Society.

Exhibitor's Full Initials, Name and Address in BLOCK LETTERS.

NAME GRIFFITH HIGH SCHOOL

ADDRESS P.O. BOX 1021
GRIFFITH 2680 N.S.W

Well-known Tamworth poultry judge, Peter Hayes, judging at Young and District Poultry Club's Annual Show, being assisted by poultry steward, Eric Bourke. A keen poultry fancier looks on.

At the same show, Peter Hayes judging a Brown Leghorn cockerel. Note the steward holding the cage open to assist the judge.

system was prone to corruption and most shows today exercise 'open judging'.

Many members of the public and particularly those new to poultry exhibiting, inquire how poultry is judged. For each breed, there is a specific written standard of perfection. Of the exhibits being judged, the fowl that, in the judge's opinion, most closely approaches the standard will be given the top award. Second prize will be given to the next best exhibit.

The standard most commonly followed in Australia is the British Poultry Standards. Some specialist breed clubs issue their own standard by which they request the breed to be judged. Other standards do exist, such as the American *Standard of Perfection*, but they are not used in this country.

As can be imagined, to be a judge, a person would have to be extremely knowledgeable about a large number of breeds. Most senior judges have themselves bred and exhibited a wide range of breeds but generally do not have any formal written judging qualifications. It is based on experience and reputation. However, attempts are now being made to formalise the training of judges and classify them according to performance at judging schools. The South Australian Poultry Association now assesses candidates in both theory and practical examinations.

At poultry shows there is a certain procedure in the allocation of awards, as follows:

Best in class
Best in variety
Best in breed
Best soft feather or hard feather
Best of heavy or light breed
Best large fowl or bantam
Best in show.

The winner at each level has its card reversed on the pen so the steward can direct the judge to the candidates for the next level of awards.

While many shows stop their awards at Best Soft Feather and Hard Feather for bantams and large fowls, people still like to know what is the 'Best bird in the show'. It is the bird that everybody visiting the poultry pavilion wants to see. The top breeders keenly seek this award.

The stewards that accompany the judge are generally members of the host club, and have the responsibility of indicating which birds the judge is to consider at each level of award allocation. Stewards also hold cage doors open so the judge can capture exhibits for handling. They record the judge's awards and write out the prize cards.

Once a fowl has been eliminated from the judging, it can be fed and watered. Wheat is a useful food for this purpose as it does not scour the bird during travelling. Water containers such as margarine containers are most practical as tins tend to rust and lower the water quality as well as causing staining.

After judging
Once the judging has been completed, the exhibitor may approach the judge to seek his comments on his own fowls as well as the other exhibits. Most judges are willing to do this provided it is done respectfully and in a courteous manner. Much can be learnt from this exercise if it is handled correctly. Nothing is achieved by publicly arguing with judges.

Presentation time
Following afternoon tea, the presentation of major awards and trophies takes place. The judges are called upon to make comments on the exhibits. Quite often they will also present major awards under the direction of the show secretary. At the conclusion of the presentations, the chief steward will permit the exhibitors to unpen their fowls for the trip home.

Taking exhibits home
It is a good idea to use your entry sheet to re-check your fowls back into their carrying boxes. This will avoid the problem of accidentally taking someone else's fowls. If you find that you have another person's fowl by accident, do the right thing and replace it in its pen and apologise to the owner. Do not stoop to steal another person's fowls, as this is regarded by the poultry fancier as one of the lowest acts.

Arrival at home
Replace the fowls in their home accommodation as soon as you arrive back from a show. Chances are they will be up, feeding and drinking before you the next morning.

Variations at agricultural shows
Birds are not unpenned until 4.30 to 5.00 p.m. in the afternoon. This irritates some fanciers but they should remember that the poultry section is only part of the overall show open to the general public. The poultry section always attracts a lot of attention and the agricultural societies see it as one of the main show attractions. Besides this, the societies build most of the pavilions used for poultry shows, charge very small entry fees and give the prize money, so they are worthy of a bit of thought from those eager to get home early. Apart from later unpenning, the show and judging format is very similar to a poultry club show.

Egg competitions
These are very popular in England, drawing up to 600 entries at some shows. In Australia, they are part of most agricultural shows and finding an increasing following in some poultry club shows. The classes vary from 6 to 12 egg exhibits in the agricultural shows down to 3 to 6 eggs in poultry club shows, which also have classes for large and bantam eggs. Most classes in egg competitions are based on colour; brown, white and other.

The presentation of the exhibit is important. Common methods used include clean egg cartons, small baskets lined with straw or plates with a bed of sawdust or shavings. Judging is based mostly on external appearance with particular attention to shape, size, shell texture, colour, freshness, bloom and general appearance. An important point to remember is evenness. Make sure the eggs are as close as possible in all the above features.

At some shows, eggs are checked for internal quality. This is generally indicated on the schedule. One of the eggs from the exhibit is broken and the following examined.

yolk albumen (white)	most importance
chalazae air space freshness	lesser importance

Keen followers of egg competitions develop special strains of fowls to lay eggs of desired show quality. Some common breeds and their egg colour are listed below:

white — Leghorn
deep brown — Welsummer, Barnevelder
brown — Rhode Island Red
other — strains of Araucanas which lay blue, green and olive eggs.

Poultry and breed clubs

Poultry Clubs

These are generally based on a particular geographical area for example:

Young and District Poultry Club (NSW)
Footscray and District Poultry Club (Vic)
Ipswich and District Poultry Club (Qld)
Adelaide Poultry Club (SA)

These cater for all breeds of fowls but can be relatively stronger in some breeds than others depending on breeder strengths and interests. Most meet on a monthly basis with the major aim of the club being to promote interest in breeding and exhibiting pure breed poultry. They are run on a voluntary basis charging their members fees to cover running costs. All endeavour to at least run an annual show each year, but many also run a young bird show early in the poultry club season to cater for the early hatchings of the previous breeding season.

Specialist breed clubs

These fit into three groups: state, national and incorporated specialist clubs.

1. State specialist clubs include such clubs as the Bantam Club of NSW and the Leghorn Club of Victoria. These draw members on a statewide basis with some coming from other states.
2. The Indian Game Club of Australia and the Ancona Club of Australia are examples of clubs that draw their membership from across the nation. Some, like the Indian Game Club of Australia, run national shows each year with exhibitors coming from all states to attend.
3. Incorporated breed clubs are specialist clubs that have been made part of another poultry club, usually because that club has a strong following of the breed of the incorporated club. An example of such a club is the Sussex Club of Australia that is incorporated into the Footscray and District Poultry Club in Melbourne.

State controlling bodies

Most poultry clubs are affiliated with a state body that is able to speak on behalf of the poultry fancy in that state. Often the state body is directly involved in the Royal Show of that state's capital. Examples of such bodies are:

Victorian Poultry Fanciers Association
All Feathered Clubs Advisory Council of NSW

Obligations of a poultry club member

1. These are voluntarily run organisations, so do not hesitate to help those who run them, or to respect them as they deserve for giving up their spare time in this way.
2. There is more to a show than the show day itself. Behind the scenes much has to be done, so when approached to help, do so rather than finding excuses to pass the buck.
3. The working bee should be a time to unify the club through some form of joint action, and the unpleasant but necessary jobs should not be left to the handful of good old club faithfuls.
4. Adopt a friendly, positive attitude as this rubs off all around and is reflected in a harmonious club.
5. Hold off criticism unless you are prepared to do something about your gripes. Talk is cheap but actions are harder to implement.

The world of the poultry fancy

The poultry fancy has a lot to offer many people. It gives a social break from the routine of ordinary life. Poultry club events are times to plan for and look ahead to. The fancier has a chance to change his surroundings and forget the everyday problems of life.

We are seeing a change in our society involving a renewed interest in growing and looking after living things. Fowls give the fancier a chance to get outside in the fresh air. Strong evidence shows that spending recreational time with other living things has a strong positive therapeutic affect on our mental health.

Opportunities exist in the poultry fancy for people of all ages to meet and share a common interest. It is a place where the young can respect the older people for their wisdom and knowledge. Older people can gain a feeling of usefulness by passing on advice based on many years of practical poultry experience, knowing that this experience will not be lost. Besides, older people feel younger when associating with the younger generation.

A network of contacts and friendships can be built up through the poultry fancy. Some of these are only renewed every twelve months or more. They are something to look forward to, adding to the social benefit of a day out at a 'chook show'. Perhaps it restores one's faith in the human race!

The challenges presented by the fancy are character builders. It is easy to be a winner but harder to be a good loser. People's character can soon be learnt by their actions, and it is not long before you find out the genuine ones, the wags and the ones to avoid. As the saying goes, 'it takes all types. . .'

11 Advice

Sources of information

Books

Most libraries carry some books on poultry, but unfortunately most of these fall into two categories which are not entirely suitable for the Australian fancier.

Books with highly technical information more applicable to the commercial side of poultry. Such books cannot be automatically dismissed as useless as they contain in depth material on poultry biology, nutrition, pests and diseases. Much of this usefully adds to your basic poultry knowledge.

Books that have been published overseas, particularly in the United Kingdom and United States of America. Provided the reader remembers the climatic as well as seasonal differences between Australia and the country of origin, pieces of useful information can be obtained. Often food materials mentioned in such books are either not available in this country or we have a better substitute.

Poultry books fit in a low volume specialist market so they are not generally stocked by large book retailers, although they can be obtained if asked for. It was for this reason that the Bantam Club of NSW started importing selected books from overseas to sell to its members. Currently, they have a comprehensive list of specialist poultry books available. Likewise, a Caringbah Pharmacist, Gerry Coady, imports and carries an impressive list of overseas books.

Magazines

Several magazines are published to serve the poultry fancy. Two examples are the *Fancier's Gazette* and the *Australasian Poultry Magazine*. They contain:

1. Specialist information on various breeds
2. Poultry health notes
3. Discussion in the form of letters to the editor
4. Show results
5. Classified advertisements for stock, egg settings and so on.

Poultry feed

Stock feed companies print and distribute information on poultry feeds. This varies from the technical through to the advertising brochure that simply explains the major differences in their range of poultry feeds. None the less, such literature is a good source of information.

Diseases

The following are three useful sources of information on diseases:

1. The experienced local poultry farmer.
2. State Department of Agriculture Poultry Officers. The Department also publishes 'Ag Fact' sheets that deal with poultry disease.
3. Your local veterinarian.

Vaccines

Arthur Webster Pty Ltd have a comprehensive range of information on vaccines, and their veterinary section will thoroughly handle any enquiries that a fancier may have on storing, preparing and administration of vaccines.

Insecticides, louse powder and worming compounds

Most of these are available in the vet or pet care section of your local pharmacy. Many agrochemical dealers also carry a range of these products to service the needs of their rural clients.

Council regulations

A phone call to your local council will inform you of council regulations in respect of keeping poultry.

Poultry facts folder

It is a good idea to have a ring folder into which information can be classified or indexed for later retrieval. Such information would include:

1. Your old show schedules so you can build up a file of poultry contacts in various areas.
2. Information written down following talking to

other fanciers. It is a good idea to carry a small note book with you when visiting shows or fellow fanciers. Jot down any useful points you may have heard. When you arrive home, write the information down and place it in your facts file.

3. Keep letters from fellow fanciers as they keep you informed of addresses and telephone numbers if you need to contact them. They also indicate their various areas of interest.

Scrapbook

From time to time, useful articles surface. These should be collected and kept in a scrapbook. To these, you can add pictures of champion birds of your chosen breed. These help you build a clearer picture of what a top fowl should look like and what you should be aiming to breed. Articles retained in a scrapbook can be re-read at a later date, when the mind is often more receptive.

Newsletters

Most breed clubs put out regular newsletters. Their quality depends on the input of the club's members and the enthusiasm of the club secretary who is saddled with the job of producing it voluntarily. The Bantam Club of NSW sends out a monthly newsletter containing minutes of their monthly meetings and useful poultry information. Other breed clubs usually send their newsletters on a quarterly basis. The Rosecomb Club is an example of a breed club that produces a most impressive quarterly newsletter.

Newspapers

Some newspapers run a poultry page. The most widely read poultry page is contained in the *Weekly Times* which also has regular photographs of show winners in its comprehensive pictorial show reports. As well, the *Weekly Times* has a well supported poultry section in its classified advertisement section.

A formula for success

This is the author's attempt to give the novice or beginner a simple formula for success which can be used with confidence, and built upon as experience grows.

Breed Selection

Select the breed that appeals to you and do not be pushed into one that you are not interested in.

Decide whether your selected breed will be utilitarian, or ornamental. Disposal of surplus utilitarian breeds is much easier than that of surplus ornamental breeds.

It is best to avoid the rarer breeds when first starting off, as stock is harder to obtain, is likely to be of doubtful quality and will receive little competition in shows. Some judges may not assess your birds well due to unfamiliarity with the breed.

Feeding

This is the largest single on-going cost associated with poultry keeping. It is best to base feeding on a commercially prepared ration to avoid any possible nutrient deficiency. The ration can be supplemented with green feed and a small amount of grain.

Pests and diseases

This will not be a problem if you have a sound poultry health care program including

proper feeding and watering

a well planned vaccination program

regular worming

dusting and spraying for external parasites.

Remember proper care with the use of chemicals when carrying out your poultry husbandry.

Housing

For the beginner, a variation of the semi-intensive system will be best.

Proper siting of the shed will also add to the fowls' comfort.

Provision must be made for show fowls, breeders, brooding of the young fowls and growing stock.

When planning your housing, check with your local council.

Breeding

Start with the best stock you can buy or obtain from a reputable breeder.

To begin with, work as a multiplier. Let a top breeder advise which birds to breed with. Once you have 'got the hang' of a breed, you can then try your own talents as a breeder.

Make sure you have a 'back up' male and female for your breeding pair or pen.

Concentrate on one or two breeds only and attempt to master them.
Try to avoid breeds that require 'double mating'.
Keep accurate records of your breeding program.
Know your breed standard.

Incubation and brooding
Broodies can be used initially but be aware of the problems associated with Marek's disease control when using them.
Ideally you should try to buy an incubator either new or second hand if you have decided that poultry raising will be a long term interest. Don't forget the brooding equipment and facilities.

Show time
Sturdy cardboard boxes will make adequate carrying boxes for you to take your fowls to a show.
It is best to take a small team of well prepared fowls rather than a large number of poorly prepared birds.
Preparation is time consuming and cannot be rushed. Good preparation enhances your fowls but is no substitute for good breeding, feeding and management.

Show day
Arrive in plenty of time for final preparation and penning.
Ask questions of judges and other fanciers but be a good listener as well.
Weigh up all points of view before forming your own opinion.

Breed clubs
Join a breed club but also be prepared to contribute to their newsletters, even if it means only passing on a few results from a show you have recently attended.

Social
With enthusiasm, the poultry fancy can be developed into a life long interest that will build a list of interesting friends and acquaintances in many parts of Australia and even overseas.

A final parting quote from Colonel P.C. Mitchell M.C. T.D., a leading British breeder, who was asked why he was such a success in the poultry fancy:

> One needs a bit of luck;
> one must try to start with good stock;
> one must learn to look and feel;
> one must realise that feeding and management can sometimes be nearly as important as breeding;
> one must read as much as possible and
> one must have enthusiasm.

Best of luck.

Poultry Clubs

New South Wales

The Bantam Club of N.S.W.
Rod Harris, Sec.
291 Galston Road
Galston 2159

Breed Clubs

The Ancona Club of Australia
M.A. O'Connor, Hon. Sec.
Box 219
Murwillumbah 2484

Federal Society of Game Fanciers
The Chairman
P.O. Box 330
Goulburn 2580

The Indian Game Club of Australia
P. Ptolemy, Hon. Sec.
58 Church Street
Cessnock 2325

The Japanese Bantam Club
Rod Harris, Hon. Sec.
291 Galston Road
Galston 2159

The Leghorn Club of Australia
Mrs B. Lord, Sec.
9 Jamieson Street
Gateshead 2240

Modern Game Club of Australia
Dale Ashton
Lot 18, Binalong Street
Murrumburra 2595

Old English Game Fanciers' Association of Australia
58 Taralga Road
Goulburn 2580

Orpington Club of Australia
Bob Lavender, Sec.
"Wirrimbirra"
Laheys Creek 2852

The Pekin Bantam Club of N.S.W.
D.J. Plant, Sec.
46 Newcastle Road
East Maitland 2323

Plymouth Rock Club of Australia
Peter Hayes, Sec.
R.M.B. 110
Tamworth 2340

The Rhode Island Club of Australia
Mrs B. Clark
288 Eighth Avenue
Llandilo 2760

Rosecomb Bantam Club
Gary R. Hart, Hon. Sec.
16 Flide Street
Caringbah 2229

Other Clubs

Coffs Harbour and District Poultry Club
Mrs S. Johns
18 Robin Street
Coffs Harbour 2450

Far North Coast All Game Club
N.T. Hing
69 Leycester Street
Lismore 2480

Forbes Pigeon and Poultry Club
Margaret Girot
P.O. Box 197
Forbes 2871

Gloucester Poultry Club
F. Beggs
15 Hay Street
Gloucester 2422

Grafton Poultry Club
Mrs B. Wilcox
Levenstrath
Grafton 2460

Inverell and District Poultry Club
Leonie Purcell
2 Hindmarsh Street
Inverell 2360

Lismore Poultry Club
J.W. Gibson
South Gundurimba
Lismore 2480

Macarthur Poultry Club
J. Parkes
P.O. Box 198
Camden 2570

Maclean Poultry Club
J.C. Watson
50 Woodford Street
Maclean 2463

Maitland Poultry Club
Mrs B. Neilson
9 Kensington Street
Bolwarra 2320

Narribri District Poultry Club
V.S. McDonald
4 Goobar Street
Narribri West 2391

Penrith Poultry Club
Sharlene Pearson, Sec.
7 Petrel Place
Tregear 2770

Sutherland/St Georges Poultry Club
F. McCarthy, Sec.
34 Ash Street
Caringbah, 2229

Tamworth Poultry Club
P.M. Smith
R.M.B. 942C
Tamworth 2340

The Central Coast Poultry Club
G.A. Garland
Lot 43, Bruce Crescent
Warnervale 2259

Tumut and District Poultry Club
Paul Donnelly
71 Broughton Street
Tumut 2720

Bellingen District Poultry Club
E. Vaughan
Elizabeth Street
Raleigh 2454

Albury Poultry Club
Andrew Scammell
157 Borella Road
Albury 2640

Cessnock District Poultry Club
Dapto Poultry Club
Ganman and District Poultry Club
Goulburn Poultry Club
Kyogle Poultry Club
Macksville and District Poultry Club
Macquarie Poultry Club
Moss Vale Poultry Club
Mudgee Poultry and Pigeon Club
Newcastle Poultry Society
Parkes Golden West Poultry Club
Parramatta and District Poultry Club
Penrith Poultry Club
South Coast Game Society
Sutherland/St. George Poultry Club
Taree Poultry Club
Wagga Wagga Poultry Club
Western Districts Hardfeather Club
Young and District Poultry Club

Canberra/Queanbeyan Poultry Club
Col Murphy, Sec.

Queensland

Beenleigh Poultry Club
Boonah Poultry Club
Bundaberg Poultry Club
Burdekin Poultry Club
Central Old Bantam Club
Charters Towers Poultry and Pigeon Club
Chinchilla Poultry Club

Far North Qld Game Fanciers club
Ken Offord, Sec.

Gympie and District Poultry and Pigeon Club
Innisfall District All Feather Club
Ipswich and District Poultry Club
Maryborough Poultry and Pigeon Club
Monto Poultry Club
Nambour Poultry Club
Oakey Bantam and Pigeon Club
Old English Game Fanciers Association of Australia
Qld Branch: Jack O'Sullivan
4 Vineyard Street
Leichhardt, Ipswich 4305
Pine RIvers Poultry Club
Rockhampton Poultry Fanciers

Mrs Lisa Silcock
240 Agnes Street
Rockhampton 4700

Roma Poultry Club
Rosewood Poultry Club
South Burnett Poultry Club
Toowoomba Feather Club
Townsville Poultry and Pigeon Fanciers Club
Tully and DIstrict All Feathers Club
Warwick Poultry Club

K.W. Schelbach
Danderoo via Warwick
Windsor Poultry Club

Victoria

Footscray and District Poultry Club
Reg Scott, Sec.
559 Geelong Road
North Altona 3025

Broadmeadows Bird Fanciers
Dan Dullard
C/- P.O. Box 76
Broadmeadows 3047

Mountain District Poultry Society
Peter Lark
29 McNicol Road
Tecoma 3160

Leghorn Club of Victoria
Neil Penny
C/- P.O. Apollo Bay 3233

Wyandotte Club of Victoria
Ray Sharpe, Sec.
Princess Highway
Pakenham 3810

Clubs affiliated with Victorian Poultry Fanciers Association

Ararat & Stawell Poultry Club
Mr A.J. Egan
Concongella via Stawell 3380

Bacchus Marsh, Melton and District Poultry Club
Mrs J. Jenkins
6 O'Neills Road
Melton 3337

Ballarat Poultry Society
Mrs H. Ronzio
Old Melbourne Road
Bungaree 3352

Bairnsdale Poultry & Pigeon Society
Mr P. Wylie
P.O. Box 662
Bairnsdale 3875

Bendigo Poultry Society
Mr A. Rilen
21 Simpsons Road
Eaglehawk 3556

Camperdown P & A Poultry Society
Mr L.G. Maslin
R.M.B. 2297
Terang 3264

Casterton-Hamilton Poultry Club
Mr I. Swaby
P.O. Box 15
Hamilton 3300

Colac Poultry Club
Mrs P. Shalley
R.M.B. AB240
Yeodene 3249

Dandenong Poultry & Kennel Society
Mr A.E. Rowney
Lot 20, Patterson Road
Cranbourne 3977

Echuca Poultry Club Inc.
Mrs L. Comer
Hills Road
Stanhope 3623

Essendon Poultry Society
Mr S.G. Anderson
18 Holyrood Avenue
Strathmore 3041

Footscray & District Poultry Society
Mr R.A. Scott
559 Geelong Road
Altona North 3025

Game Club of Victoria
Mr J. Eastes
9 Mirabel Avenue
Ringwood East 3135

Geelong & District Poultry Club Inc.
Mr I. Grant
5 Twitt Street
Newcomb 3219

Hamburgh Club of Australia
Mr K. Mason
Gibbs Road
Healesville 3777

Kerang & District Pigeon & Poultry Club
Mrs L. Chalmers
"Four Winds"
Wakool NSW 2710

Leghorn Club of Victoria
Mr N. Penny
12A McLachlan Street
Apollo Bay 3233

Mountain District Poultry Society
Mr P. Lark
29 McNicol Road
Tecoma 3160

Northern All Game Poultry Club
Mrs Satchell
9 Sovereign Court
Eaglehawk 3556

Oakleigh District Poultry Society
Mr D. Simpson
37 Fintonia Road
Noble Park 3174

Peninsula Poultry Fanciers Club
Mr I. Earle
P.O. Box 30
Baxter 3911

Victorian Poultry & Kennel Club
Mr W. Burnell
86 Railway Place
Williamstown 3016

Victorian Rare & New Breed Society
Mr K. Smith
42 Maude Street
Box Hill North 3129

Whittlesea & District Poultry Club
Mr W. Bickerton
Group 7, 14th Avenue
Eden Park 3757

Whittlesea Agricultural Society Inc.
P.O. Box 83,
Whittlesea 3757

Wimmera Poultry Club
Mrs J. Laverty
R.M.B. 321
Nhill 3418

Wyandotte Club of Victoria
Mr R.J. Sharpe
Princes Highway
Pakenham 3810

South Australia

South Australian Poultry Association Inc.
Adrian Kuys
Sanderston. R.S.D. via Palmer 5237

Adelaide Poultry Club
All Fanciers Poultry Club
Bantam Club of S.A.
Gawler District Poultry Club Association
Lobethal Poultry Club
Poultry and Kennel Club of S.A.
Mid North Poultry Club
Murray Bridge Poultry and Pigeon Club
Southern Districts Poultry Club
Wyandotte Club of S.A.
York Peninsula Poultry and Pigeon Club

Western Australia

West Australian Poultry Association
Mrs M. Harman, Sec.
162 Franklin Road
Wanneroo 6065

South West Poultry Association
Mr Bruce Fellows, Sec.
R.M.B. 248
Busselton 6280

Harvey & Districts Poultry Association
Mr Jim Rake, Sec.
1 Sir James Avenue
Harvey 6220

Midland Poultry Association
Mr Geoff Blinco, Sec.
23 Bushby Street
Midvale 6056

Avon Poultry Association
Mr Jim Fuller, Sec.
141 Avon Terrace
York 6302

Esperance Poultry Association
Mr David Boydell, Sec.
Napier Road
Esperance 6450

Albany Poultry Association
Mrs Barbara Blechynden, Sec.
R.M.B. 197
Mt Manypeaks via Albany 6330

Narrogin & Districts Poultry Association
Mr L.B. Rowley, Sec.
George Street
Narrogin 6312

Tasmania

Burnie Poultry Society
D. Haywood, Sec.
12 Cannon Court
Burnie 7320

Poultry Club of Tasmania
B. Bennett, Sec.
3A Clare Street
Hadspen 7254

Bantam Club of Tasmania
D. Henderson, Sec.
56 Neika Avenue
Launceston 7250

Southern Tasmanian Poultry Club
M. McMaster, Sec
38A Coleman Street
Moonah 7009

Southern Tasmanian Bantam Club
D. Ward, Sec.
37 Bedford Street
Newton 7008

Hobart Rhode Island and Sussex Club
D. Rowberry, Sec.
26 Charles Street
Moonah 7009

North West Poultry Society
Robert Walsh, Sec.
R.S.D. Reservoir Drive
Wynyard 7325

Game Club of Tasmania
Robert Walsh, Sec.
R.S.D. Reservoir Drive
Wynyard 7325

Devonport Poultry Club
M. Lucas, Sec.
11 Archer Street
Devonport 7310

Index